THE SOVEREIGN SEALS
OF GOD AND GODDESS
PART ONE

By
Ben Aster

BLUE HOUSE BOOKS
Baltimore 2021

Dedication

Revealing the Sovereign Seals of God and Goddess is an honor. May those that I have learned from, continue to learn from, have taught and continue to teach be blessed by my actions.

The author's obligations common to all were enough to rise to the occasion of the discovery of the most important revelation of our time. With conscious faith, working love, and hope in salvation, the good that can come from revealing the Sovereign Seals, to the world's people, may ease the suffering of those who though recently born are nonetheless living in the last day before the new. Have heart, the new day begins a new age!

To those of the past who have given of themselves to make possible the revelation of the Sovereign Seals, and to those who are alive, who themselves are a part of those present, who are living for the sake of future generations, I write this book for you. We must be careful. The world is fragile, no matter how enduring we might think Earth and Heaven is, they are all connected. We often forget that we are in Heaven because we are on Earth with all the fancy things, but Earth is in Heaven as you will discover while reading this book.

The author intends to assist the Author Living dreaming into reality a gift from Our Common Mother and Father. They are and have been constants in the life of the author and are my oldest friends. May peace be with Them.

The Sovereign Seals of the Most High God and Goddess is not for JHVH, Allah or any other "named" being because there is no name we can give the Most High. Each of us carries our own name for the Being. The Most High is not the God of anyone anywhere, but the God of everyone everywhere. By name the Most High is believed in but not known. All who know God as Nameless, know nothing came before to give God a name. The miracle lives, free.

Two thousand years ago, if Jesus could have revealed the Sovereign Seals, certainly he would have shared them. Scripture implies, only after all of the prophesied things happened to Jesus, from birth to crucifixion to resurrection, he proved his worth to God, our worth, and put into scripture the Sovereign Seals, written as a vision, a revelation to John.

Gratefully, some of us abide and share stories of the shocking things in life. The stories with the greatest shock value arouse more than a passing interest in our average mundane lives. Otherwise, the mundane is enough to drive anyone crazy. History is the craziness of normal insane people taking a few notes.

Jesus, knowing our state, was moved to believe in himself, God, and us. The book of a Revelation to John, the 66th and last book of the Bible has been driving scholars crazier than anything else because A Revelation juxtaposes the two opposing themes, salvation and death. The world is destroyed and saved from destruction repeatedly. The New Testament begins with John the Baptist, prior to Jesus's commission, declaring that the kingdom of Heaven draws near. Then, Jesus declares that the kingdom of Heaven is here, then and now.

Epigraph

And God has placed his mark upon our forehead.

"And I saw another angel ascending from the sunrising, having the seal of the living God; and he cried to the four angels . . .3 saying: 'Do not harm the earth or the sea or the trees, until after we have sealed the slaves of our God in their forehead.", A Revelation 7:2.

Are we beasts to be scarred by numbers? Beasts take responsibility for their own kind and sometimes other kinds. Are we beastly but also divine? Maybe we are the Divine Beasts? If that title finds us taking care of all the other beasts in common cause like life and the salvation of the world's future, then we are already hearing the tune at the heart of nature and at the heart of our nature.

Two omni-prescient Realities Exist in scripture. First is the Seal of God's Sovereignty, which this book is about, and the second is the mark of the seal of God, the Alpha and Omega. The Bible tells us God is the Alpha and Omega. Rev. 22:13, "I am the Alpha and the Omega, the first and the last, the beginning and the end."

The mark of God on our foreheads is almost invisibly resting upon the brows. All members, male and female, of the "human" race have the Omega mark. It extends from the eyebrows to the hairline of the forehead. There are at least a few scriptures that talk about a mark on the forehead or the hand. The scriptures most related to the mark of God found in the book of A Revelation, seems to be derived in essence from the Old Testament prophet Ezekiel, chapters 9 and 10, which describe a mark on the forehead and also beings with more than one face that were definitely not human in appearance.

Early Greeks chose the image Omega for the last letter of their alphabet, the letter 'O'. Omega, the last letter, is also the first number, zero, a word that amounts to nothing but from which one is derived, begins with the letter 'z' and rhymes with the word hero. Within the symbol for zero, a circle exists, where every everything relative to the absolute, the full accompaniment of all things, are geometrically derivable, meaning all things as One, God the Creator cosmologically and philosophically. The reason that the circle is a letter, number, and universal symbol is because it reflects the possibility of the relative knowledge of the absolute in the only way that we or any other species of such vast creative potential can respond to truthfully. The circle does not represent chaos but order, The Order. The teaching of the Sovereign Seal is to reveal how from the circle comes all things, from the One and nothing, how form becomes manifest. Forms have surfaces and they must arise somehow. How does a circle or circles create form such as triangular forms, squares, pentads, hexagons, atomic and cosmic structure from a circle? Motion? And what provokes motion? Will? Inspiration? Love? Some say loneliness or fear made motion begin. Some philosophers have boiled it all down to one prime move. What is your best pick-up line?

On the forehead of every living breathing human being is scribed the mark of God. The Omega symbol given to us by our historic Greek brethren fits on the faces of all people. We the people, you, are made perfect in the image of God and Goddess. The source image for the perfection of Humanity comes from the tectonically resonating landmass called Africa. Tectonic Resonant Evolution, my first book, theorizes that the macro-cosmic image of Africa is the source image for the human skull. The sign of God upon our common facial images, the Omega Symbol, appears in our common source image where the Red Sea was cut.

God's Alpha Mark

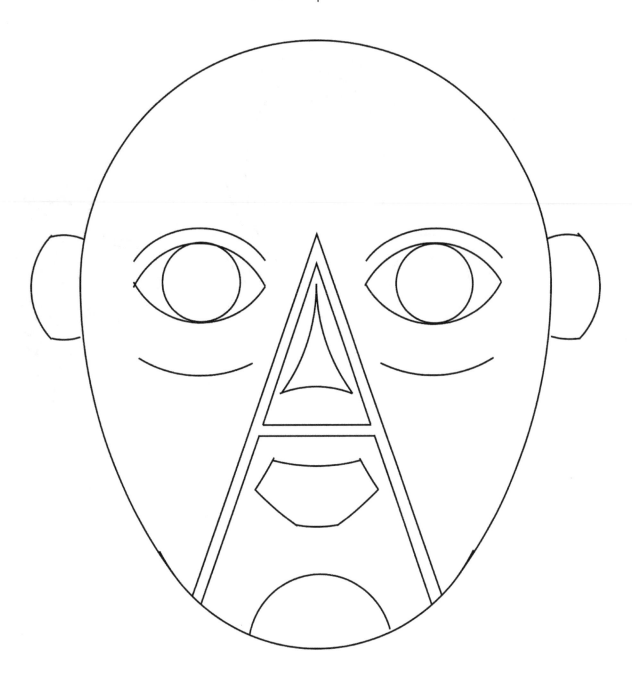

God's perfection manifests in the geometrical perfection of the Alpha Mark. The Alpha mark is a tool to describe a circle, a compass caliper. Job 26:10 "He has described a circle upon the face of the waters."

Goddess's Omega Mark

The Omega Mark is s geometrical expression of the divine feminine.
The words that brought forth creation were not "Let there be light."
The word was, "Push!"

Africa the God Skull

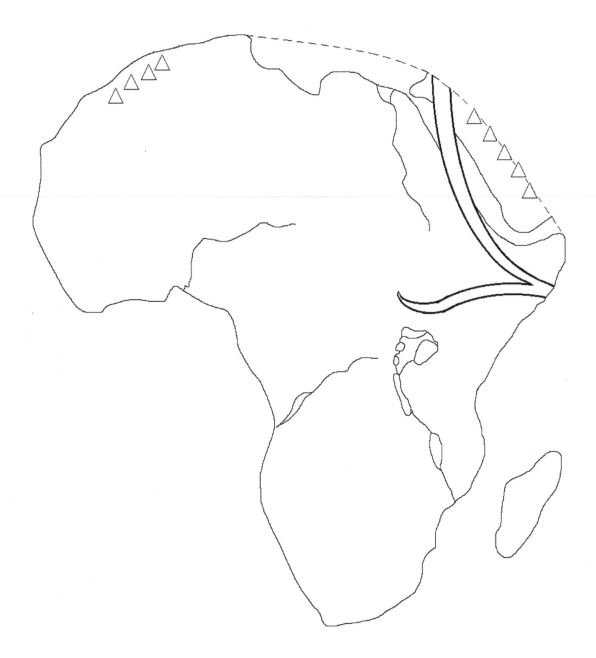

The Omega Mark as macrocosmic expression of the divine.

Contents

<u>Acknowledgments</u>

I hear the children of the future crying out. They approach in the spirit from a distant place and as they get closer, I can see them clearly, tens of thousands of children, their voices sound like a morning flock of birds all chirping together saying the same thing over and over again, "You could have at least tried." I hear you children of the future, "I am trying.".

The information you are about to receive in the book was given to me to give to you and is only part of the knowledge as a whole. I have a lifetime's worth of work ahead of me, to reveal a lifetime's worth of research. The depth and scope of the research extends through history, space, time and can fill a small library.

I, the author, received a large treasure trove of research. This book you are about to read is a compilation of the handwritten research gifted me and does not reflect the entirety of the research. I did my best to retain as much of the original handwritten research as possible. However, I did have to edit some of the original research for the purpose of this book.

The originator of the source material pleaded with me saying, "Please help me publish my research before I die. The most important thing you can do with your life is to go through my research, pull out my best material, and do the best you can to save the world with what I have given you."

I asked myself, "If the afterlife is eternal and all we have is our memories for eternity, how am I choosing to remember my life?" Many thoughts passed quickly through my head. The thought that spoke the loudest said, "I don't want to live in regret remembering for eternity not doing something I know I should do." I answered the call, like all heroes do, and published my first book Tectonic Resonant Evolution. All references to the word 'I' and 'author' no longer refers to me as the author, but to the individual who granted me their research and the wonderful opportunity to share it with you.

Entrusted was I, and I have passed the sacred trust to Ben Aster. This book is written with the expressed purpose of intentionally revealing or unveiling the Most Holy and Most Sacred of all objective truths to the people of Earth. Writing this book is an action understood as the sacred duty of yours truly.

With the help of a genuine friend, the author, co-acting under spiritual compulsion, commonly called "the promise of God", we offer this resolve, the Sovereign Seals revelation, to fulfil our common cosmic order. Peace be with you, always.

Prologue

Religion is belief.
Belief is agreement.
Agreement is bond.
Bond is trust.
Trust is love.
Love is family.
Family is oneness multiplied,
Adding more and more
To the multiples of oneness,
Yet, remaining one.

"Whoever does the will of God, this one is my brother and sister and mother.", Mark 3:35.

The Sovereign Seal is not likely a truth that we can agree to disagree about, and just let it go. God's mark, the Sovereign Seal, is the very gravity that holds Heaven and Earth as One. In law, the Sovereign has jurisdiction. In law, the Sovereign rules. So, upon this rock I waited, playing the guitar weeping. The thunders came to talk it over, they thundered, "Why do you wait?"

Wiping the rain off of my guitar with my shirt I thundered back gracefully, "I am too scared! I should wait for Jesus!"

Time went by. Jesus began to appear with the thunders through a mandorla that was opening in front of me like some magic portal. The guitar I was playing dropped to the floor with an unmelodious clang which shocked whoever was about to appear. As the mandorla closed it exploded, and the thunders hammered the house like Thor.

So, while we are waiting patiently for Jesus, I might as well prepare him some room, and prepare the rest of you for the Second Coming or his big return, by disclosing the device he will use to prove his claim: The Sovereign Seal of God the Father, and the Sovereign Seal of Goddess the Mother. You probably wouldn't believe me if I told you Both are virgins and that creation exists within the bliss of Their first moments together.

Seals go farther back than Hermes and Thoth. Both of them have an airtight alibi. They were waiting for Jesus, too. They were probably well-aware of the sacred secret, but they too had to wait for the Messiah. No one had ever passed all the tests of Satan, and Jesus's last test of faith was the cross. The texts give us the belief that at some point Jesus ascended to the right hand of God and was given the Scroll of the Seven Seals, proving his worth as he took the Scroll of the Seals.

After Jesus's departure, the Apostles spoke of the sacred secret seal on various occasions, but by then, they were already waiting for the Second Coming. The sacred secret remained so secret that we lost it altogether.

The histories of religions, philosophies, and just plain old history, proves that mankind, by and large has no idea, of Goddess or God. Often, I have thought, if only humanity had received the Sovereign Seal before they did so much harm to the world, what would that world be like? Most of man's behavior could be defined as insane, causing harm to themselves and others, and that is humanity's basic history, becoming more increasingly difficult to shake the memories of all the evil they've witnessed or perpetrated on creation, others, and themselves. Abuses to nature are also offensive to God.

God and Goddess are living, but They remain hidden for reasons. On the rarest occasion when one or the other does appear, the people would sacrifice large quantities of animals, to feed the giant God in the sky and sometimes people too, for some thought God might be a cannibal. All of those insane animal sacrifices in the Old Testament happened. Often depicted at those awful activities are beings who fail to fit the definition of angelic, though they often wore a lot of feathers. Those who were in tune with Goddess and the real God, were hunted. The more peaceful peoples were usually easier prey for brutish regimes.

The real Goddess and real God would never ask for any kind of sacrifices or even worship.

Before my bones wore too thin to travel I occasionally did. On one of my journeys, I had a vision from Our Heavenly Mother of Her chosen sons, and the seals Her sons gave their people. In one arm was the Great Book born by Our Common Mother. I never got the chance to see inside Her book. In Her other arm there was a bundle of flowers. From the centers of the flowers came the faces of very historically significant persons, Her sons, each was given a symbol. First the person's face appeared and faded back into the center of the flower. Then the person's symbol appeared and faded back into the center, from which reemerged the face of Her chosen sons.

Fourteen months prior I had been in a horrific automobile crash, died repeatedly, returned, and spent what seemed like a long time conversing with the 'dead', which is a whole other story. The vision of Our Heavenly Mother led to complete introspection, the cause of all done, a truth sewn into the spirit of the fabric of my being, all being, a semi-conscious inner divinity was and is seeking truth through the process of questioning everything through life which could examine truth. The truth being created in our automata seeks to be at peace, sifts through all experience, studies all, and creates the resolve, a universe in one's own world which per scale might be held and studied further for cosmological perspectives. Undertaken was a study of everything on all scales.

Late in the Summer of 1980, I was expounding on an important theme while living in Las Vegas, New Mexico. At about 3:30 A.M. I was theorizing the basement universe theory, banging my head up against the primordial axioms when I wrote what Immanuel Kant would call an antithesis of reason. Scholars claim that what qualifies God as the Creator, is because He is the First Cause Uncaused, the Prime Mover. Around the apartment all of the books were laid out, all the philosophies and religious texts were open, and I had just written the second axiom of my assumptions.

The first axiom of my assumptions was that we question because at the root of life itself within us is a divine spirit that is seeking peace with the creation and thus the knowledge of everything external to the body. At the end of my assertion was, that man would study all things on all scales relative to his existence, and then, create a universe on his own scale of existence such that he could place a universe on his dining room table as a centerpiece, observe, study, and draw conclusions about the possible end of our universe, and thus man would no longer be man by definition, but a god, filling a niche between infinite micro-creative powers and infinite macro-creative powers.

Earlier, that year in the middle of the night, on the nineteenth of February, was when I wrote my first axiom. I was staying at my father's place. The door to my room was closed and locked. Pink Floyd's "The Wall" was on the turntable and the wall was coming down.

Lightning flashed outside the window. The thunder struck close. The locked door to the room opened. A bright hot white light body entered the room and telepathically told me to reread what I had written: That "in the end" man would not be man, but a maker of a universe, a god. The light faded as the record came to an end and the storm faded.

I had not yet dotted the final sentence with a period when lightning struck, as if to shout, "Yes! Somebody has finally figured it out!" That is what I heard the thunder say as the locked door began to open. When the echoes of what the thunder voiced ascended into the heavens, every star in the universe heard the word. At the center of the Milky Way Galaxy the light got a whole shade more brilliant in color and a vibrational grace of peace and honor emanated from the center throughout the entire universe, as if to say, "thank God", for throughout the entire universe, with all of the intelligences out there, here, and throughout the entirety of the universe's existence, no one had ever dared to conceive through introspection beyond the veil, to a Creator, much like Jesus, John, or you, could become a "Creator God". The Basement Universe Theory was the result from the introspection developed from the external experience of seeing the Great White Spirit Mother Goddess about seven months before, with the book and the flowers with the seals and their messengers.

The night in Las Vegas, when I wrote my second axiom, I wrote, "The reason that "God", cannot be the Creator, the first cause uncaused is because, the first rule of causation or the law of nature, of motion, of God, is also the law of change, which boldly declares, "Nothing is ever the cause of itself." At the moment I finished writing that very sentence, I heard from behind me, a voice that sounded like a trumpet blast, so loud that I was certain the whole world had to have heard that voice. The words like thunder shook my bones and through me rumbled the aged watery voice of God the Father, in the dead of night saying, "Mark me down." I didn't stop shaking until I met the Old Fellow, God Almighty, during a blizzard at midday, when I was beginning to fulfil my sworn oath. However, as He appeared, I was ordered to bow down by an angelic male voice. I could not. My cold nearly frozen wet legs were locked at the knees, besides, to bow down before anyone, God or Devil, would have been "Un- American". Eyes to eyes locked, the strength of Heaven's God warmed me, and I finally stopped trembling, for my bones were quaking well over a year, since the night in Las Vegas, when He said, "Mark me down." When I turned, He turned, and I am still not absolutely sure, but, I think, He might be quietly agreeing that, though He is God, Almighty, and all of that thundering throne of the Heavenly Host stuff, the basement universe theory thing, might still have some legs to stand on.

John writes in the book of A Revelation 1:10, "By inspiration I came to be in the Lord's day, and I heard behind me a strong voice like that of a trumpet, 11 saying: "What you see write in a scroll and send it to the seven congregations, in Ephesus and Smyrna and in Pergamum and in Thyatira and in Sardis and in Philadelphia and in Laodicea." God's voice sounds like a man trying to speak and drink water at the same time, like many waters, because He is ancient, and according to the book of Genesis, reality responds directly to His voice.

Verse 14 tells us, "Moreover, his head and his hair were white as white wool, as snow, and his eyes as a fiery flame;" Verse 15, "and his feet were like fine copper when glowing in a furnace; and his voice was as the sound of many waters." The voice of God sounds like a trumpet blast, which sets men's bones to quaking. Perhaps ancient man got the idea that there is water above the firmament because when God speaks His voice also sounds like He is drowning.

In Isaiah 66:1, "This is what JHVH has said: "The heavens are my throne, and the earth is my footstool. Where, then, is the house that you people can build for me, and where, then, is the place as a resting place for me?"

Matthew Chapters 5, 6, & 7, is the famous Sermon on the Mount where in verses 34-35 Jesus says, "I say to you: Do not swear at all, neither by heaven, because it is God's throne; nor by earth, because it is the footstool of His feet;". The image of God and the world held by the prophets is repeated throughout scripture. Verse 48 says: "You must accordingly be perfect, as your heavenly Father is perfect." The Sovereign Seals are perfect too.

On my journey through the gates of beauty, poverty, frustration, and exhaustion, there was God stepping in without leaving His throne to give me His perspective while on a prolonged vision quest in winter's grip. Fifteen years passed and I was recuperating from many injuries when I finally had the time, so I began The Holy of Holies teaching, returning to the vision of Our Heavenly Mother, specifically drawing the mandala seals that were inside the centers of the flowers bundled in Her left arm, like Buddha's lotus, Lao Tzu's Yin and Yang, Mohammed's crescent Moon and Sun and Jesus's fish-like sigil.

While on my journey through those gates I stumbled into sacred geometry, in which every line has value, lawful, universal, mathematical, virtue. I moved through the sequences circle by circle until I drew the Sovereign Seal of God. Before I had fully recognized the image I had drawn, I was ordered to put it away. The next days I was so furiously attacked by something invisible twisting my bones and throwing me across the room, that I could barely move. Each breath was a singular event.

I have not got a religion to invent. That stopped after I was told to put my research away by an angelic feminine voice with a body invisible to the naked eye. I stopped right then and there and put the whole teaching of numerical exploration away. A few years later, a dear friend of mine came to me, after having a fourth heart attack and said, "I was instructed by the dead to come and tell you to re-open and examine your work on the drawings of artistic numerical exploration of sacred geometry." After rereading the book of A Revelation to John I recognized that I had drawn the Sovereign Seals. Now, I do not know what to do. Maybe I am first to have drawn and recognized the Sovereign Seals for over a thousand years.

My eventful life left me with a broken back, pneumonia, cancer and a multitude of other obligations. The world was coming to an end for me, so, I reread A Revelation for the hundredth time. The seven stars jump out of the first chapter which was where I left off. After reading A Revelation 12:1, I retrieved a compass, paper, protractor, and the Seal of the Goddess leaped forth in its glory, with twelve stars.
James 1:12, "Happy is the man that keeps on enduring trial, because on becoming approved he will receive the crown of life, which JHVH promised to those who continue loving him."

Anyone schooled in scripture like the Bible will tell you in a word or two that our history reads like a bloody battle. We can blame everything but our salvation, on the Devil and still have nary a clue. Scripture speaks of war between the forces of good and evil, where the evil ones did everything possible to keep us from ever seeing the Sovereign Seal or hearing about it. There has been a very long multi-generational battle where the forces of evil were so efficient and successful that we had little idea about the issue of God's Sovereignty. Our beliefs in individual rights, as sovereign individuals, gave us a sense of freedom to reject subjugation and oppose suffering under the rule of a monarch or theocrat.

The Sovereign Seal is the very symbol of triumph over the forces of evil who had been successful in bringing the human race's existence into an ungodly unbelievable nightmare, that became the twentieth century A.D. How did the evil one's manage to keep the Sovereign Seals out of human hands until now? Was humanity being tested as scripture suggests?

Why would the gods test the human race and why use beings who were so malevolent that other angels exiled them, to our world? Were the evil one's exiled on Earth as punishment? Once they were isolated to the planet Earth, instead of abroad wreaking havoc, they were probably left to resort to their own devices, on Earth.

There are some myths that imply after a rebellion in Heaven there were many angels banished or exiled on Earth. Over time, many of the angels repented and could return to their heaven or their home planet. Those who refused to repent involved themselves in manipulating the human species. The Great Flood of Noah's time was Our Heavenly Father's attempt to wipe out as many as He could of the unrepenting 'fallen angels' and their genetic monstrosities, as both are unable to assimilate into the spirit of heaven here. These hybrid horrors, the Nephilim are as a virus to our God in Heaven.

Apparently, there were only a few, three or four, who survived the Deluge, who had the power to appear as many. Though not human or angel, the fallen angels and hybrid horrors could appear to us as angels of light. In myth the fallen angels created the human race only to make us, as slaves, to assist in some hidden agenda, to use us to assist them, the fallen ones, in their endeavors to free themselves from the surface of the Earth and invade their old home planet, where they need to be in order to transubstantiate their own spirits for assimilation of their kind into the heavenly fabric of eternal spirit into their original place of conception, so they, can be eternal in spirit, from the moment of their death. I doubt the fallen ones ever disclosed where they originated from, only pointing to various stars.

Perhaps the story of the fallen angels explains why the human race is never visited by peoples of other worlds. They do not want to take any chance of dying off world or any chance of some 'fallen angel' like Satan, who can literally shapeshift, appear, disappear, and possess weaker minds, escaping back into the heavens on one of those spaceships. Might the Sovereign Seal be a passport allowing for travel and transport on trans-space- ships, a requirement for spaceflight? Are the Seals of God and Goddess a Sacred Trust for Heaven's star people?

For a quarter century I have been celebrating, very privately, the victory over the evil ones and the recovery or discovery of the Sovereign Seal which happened at the same time. My service was pivotal, for I was sensed at a very young age. The evil one's knew I was aware of them. That is a story the words for which are few for me. The real heroes are parental and family co-sufferers, but even more than we, are the heroes you may know from their actions which human history records. John the Baptist, Jesus and his apostles, and quite a few others laid everything on the line to defeat these unrepentant fallen angels whose villainous pride knew no bounds.

Every great civilization had heroes that died because they were killed by the evil ones trying to use humanity's existence as a ransom to bring all of

Heaven to a state of constant sorrow, using us, to punish Heaven. The story gets all gory. Read our world history and see for yourselves, how a few devils were overtly and more recently covertly denying humanity their divinity and offering us a bowl of soup for our birthright after starving humanity from recognizing God and God's love for us all as His Children.

The telling of some stories is unnecessary, too painful to be forced to recall just to wet someone's imagination with false senses of self. When Satan perished there was a celebration in Heaven. Most surprising to me was that the celebration was about as brief as a common television commercial advertisement. The Devil's death meant his kind would come for his remains and kill anybody who tried to stop them, even if they had to wipe out humanity. About three thousand people died the day Satan's skull was retrieved by his people.

We are waking up from the dream that was God's nightmare for more than a few of His days. I would say your guess is as good as mine. Jesus was going to use the Sovereign Seals to found the kingdom of Heaven on Earth, two thousand years ago. Just as one might keep their lamenting to a minimum, so they do not die of misery, so Heaven holds its rejoicing to a minimum.

Only time will tell how the people will see themselves now that the Sovereign Seal is with us. How will the future look? Will the Sovereign Seals be interpreted as a sign from God? Time was short for Satan and is even shorter for us, before Heaven will take judicious action and implore the people to react in harmony with what the Seal perfectly reveals.

Preface

Heaven is on Earth and Earth in Heaven. They seem like separate worlds, but they aren't. Earth is where you live, where we all live. From Heaven, on Earth I bring to you, by location, live, The Sovereign Seals. This book, The Sovereign Seals of God and Goddess Part One, renders a sacred service to those looking down from above and those looking around, up from below. The Sovereign Seals are new to the people of Earth and will shift them into the cosmic consciousness common to those conscious of their divinity.

Like a seed, an idea, the Sovereign Seals is sown into the soil of yesterday, a soil that needs to be turned over and loosened. The seed is planted and watered. Then, we must be patient and wait. If the good Earth receives and Heaven blesses the seed of our salvation, then the seed may sprout. This seed may be the most important of all seeds sowable. So, protect it! Our ancient ancestors sought and spoke of, in their great myths, and religious stories about a sign from God. The Sovereign Seals, the seed, comes from God and Goddess, connecting us to Them, and is Their insignia, Their Sign.

The building of a more permanent godly spiritual way for consecutive generations, requires that this book breaks ranks with all academia and ecclesia, who are focused on the retention of power knowledge controls. There is a new, physical and spiritual metaphysical truth that can save us from the dead science that academia is mired in, internationally, politically, and economically, called the Sovereign Seals.

Verse four of chapter one, the book of A Revelation to John reads, "John to the seven congregations in the district of Asia: May you have undeserved kindness and peace from "The One who is and who was and who is coming."", is a quote within a quote. "The One", is the Cosmic One, the Creator of the Universe, the First Being of Creation was considered an ordinal progression from nothingness to all that Creation is today, when created time and being came to be in existence. The One has the power to commune with a part of itself that is in all things, galaxies, stars, planets, people, plants, animals, and everything everywhere. So, when the One communes with a person, all that the person needs to do is commune with the One within themselves, unless instructed otherwise by the One.

A person uses mandalas to assist in communing with the One, while meditating in silence, without distraction or intention. Ancient disciplines from all over the world have had the goal of teaching parents to teach their children to be quiet, and in the stillness of the quietness learn to commune with the One within themselves. Teaching silence was done as a precaution, so that if ever, for whatever reason, the parents might not be at hand momentarily their children do not "freak out". They stay calm, wait, and listen to what the One within themselves is saying.

Recognizing the One in themselves children progress to recognizing the One in all things, as adults. Some progress on to assisting the One which is a service rendered as sacred service. Moses must have ironically realized the meaning of service when he called himself "God's slave" while freeing the Israelites in the Exodus. By the assisting of others, following "the Golden Rule", the actions of the One and the Heaven of the One is recognized and dutifully tended to. The One rules Heaven, and the human race will never be free until they realize the cornerstone, "All Serve."

No one is free. Does the Sun just get up and walk off? Freedom exists within the laws of possibility, but all possibility only exists in the limits of God's laws, like the natural cosmic mathematical laws governing creation.

How long can you hold your breath before God's Law says, "Breathe"? If you do not, you die, and you can no longer serve in the world of the Living God. The assisting of others is the assisting of God, and when we do, we have done God's Will, and that action is called an act of love. The abuse of the Golden Rule is intolerable and tyrannical. Love builds like a carpenter.

Some things are perfect, like everything. Not realizing the perfection of things has caused harm to come to the world that is currently hosting our complete and total existence. Harm has come to the people and all other living creatures of the planet, all of which are created by the One. The oath of the people should be no different than that of Hippocrates, the healer, "First, do no harm."

And people, just because you have been given this final rose, The Sovereign Seals, does not mean continue messing up the world. Stop trying to cross a rickety rope bridge with a Sherman tank just because you want to cross the river. Stop trying to cross the D.N.A. of a pterodactyl with a whale, crocodile, and an anaconda, just because you think you can create something, "Really cool!" The realization that one's own life is a living miracle of the One, on Earth, in Heaven, is a good enough realization to feel good about every day, every breath, no matter how bad the day gets.

The true work of a master is developing their own permanent, eternal, crystalized and resonating "I", a complete sense of one's being essence or soul, spirit, ego, logos, that might survive death for a while, and maybe forever.

The sages teach that a complete sense of self is the ultimate goal in life which includes death, meaning life is not concerned with the accumulation of wealth or knowledge, or the mechanical prolonging of life, but solely in the perfecting of one's eternal soul.

Knowledge of self was the original apex of the great schools and disciplines of the highest order designed to assist others in the most rapid development of the accumulating of spiritual goodness, to free those disciplined to assist in God's work, consciously and intentionally assisting Him in a more permanent arrangement for His blessings on future generations.

When the work is being done and the religions realized, belief will no longer be necessary, nor disbelief a choice. The religions born of man die and are reborn as a higher state of being, a state of knowing, called gnosis, conscience, constant awareness of place and time. Nirvana, the path of sages, leads to liberation as an end result, that the people will eventually remember, and reach freedom. The process is a quest, a question, and the ability to answer depends upon the protection of the freedom to do so.

The rule of the master is to head up the teaching of others, which means to make the school's participants to be aware and to pay attention to everything going on around themselves and within themselves at all times. The exercise of correct schooling teaches alertness, meaning to pay attention, as the first principle. How many times did your teachers have to ask you or your classmates to pay attention?

One of the main fundamentally misunderstood experiences is the prophetic dream, a manifestation blamed as a first cause of a déjà vu, is a direct manifestation of our ability, a Divine Ability of the subconscious autonomic aspect of the mind, brain, soul, to pre-perceive one's self in a dream before the event has come to pass. Even little animals dream. Whether you are a macrocosmic being or a lesser cosmic being like one of us, the scale of one's being doesn't seem to matter. Maybe all beings have manifestations of themselves in their own subconscious, and can access a state of prescient knowing, seeing and hearing, experiencing events that have not yet taken place. Prophetic dreaming seems impossible according to the laws of physics, yet, everybody can, even God. God must've had a really long prophetic dream for the book of His revelation is twenty-two chapters.

If the Heavenly Mother and Father didn't love each other then creation would be nothing but a universal constant state of sin. Our cosmic parents are in the process of Their first time: Their First Kiss, Their First Hug. Their First Orgasms are quietly creating the energy seeding the heaven with the stars and the Earth with every kind of soul. Each has a consciousness no matter the scale of Being. However, in the proper working of the subconsciousness, what to us is apparently reality is one part of the whole. The soul has the innate ability to prophetically dream, from which a prescient vision can occur. Prophetic dreaming is different from having a vision of God on His Throne in which all the angels appear to us when our eyes are open while we are conscious and consciously participating in being instructed. Mother Earth appears as you would appear in a dream. She is dreaming a dream we call reality.

There is a type of dream people have, where in the dream, they see themselves sleeping, and then, they merge with that image and have a dream, a dream within a dream. Recurring dreams are nearly identical all of the way to the end where you find a new solution. Children have dreams of themselves as adults, and when older, dreams of youth. There are dreams from a whole octave higher of objective reality being viewed as if you are being watched, and you discover you are watching yourself from a higher plane of perspective. You turn to see what you are looking at, and what you see is a happy long-forgotten memory from a place a thousand years in the future. Imagine, Mother Nature has kept track of Her living dream with all living things, including seven billion human souls.

The book of a Revelation explains that God had a vision of future times, a prophetic dream. If God has a vision, a prophetic dream, possibly a dream of His self in His future, His prescient vision comes from an objective third point of perspective in time, a future time. Even for God His time and life are real. He is aging. Is there then, an even higher eternal objective point of perspective in the consciousness of God, a soul in His soul, that is in scale, Mega-lo-cosmic, a consciousness that is God warning God, with a vision in the form of a prescient dream?

This book on the Sovereign Seals is to be used to provide its revelation, an apocalypse of God, to assist in the healing of broken souls, spirits, hearts, and bodies, and remind us of our perfection and divinity which we might be able to master singularly as individuals, in group work, and perhaps even a world working together consciously, for a more perfect permanent sense of ourselves as a world people, as one people. For, if we are able to be masters of our own domain, we should learn to master ourselves, at which time we may approach the real Master of this Domain.

To my knowing, the people of Earth, of which I am one, had never seen the Sovereign Seals before. Throughout the centuries of human history, the shamanic myths, legends, and histories reveal that only a few were shown, by angelic messengers, bits and pieces of the Sovereign Seals. We will look at the history of those bits and pieces, called sigils or seals, which compose the Sovereign Seals. The individuals who were used for the purpose of revelation were probably looking for answers, intensely searching for truth, salvation, and meaning, some signpost to the lost key of the lost treasure. However, to say that the key and treasure were lost would imply they are missing, that they were here somewhere, maybe over there? And then, sometime later, the treasure and key were gone, not there.

There were only pieces and previous descriptions of pieces of paradise, maps, legends of immortals, gods and goddesses. The main source of the descriptions by people about the pieces is scripture. Scripture tells us about the bits and pieces. This scripture, the Sovereign Seals of God and Goddess Part One, is mostly found in bits and pieces throughout the scriptures known as the Bible, predominantly described in the last book, the book of a Revelation, also called the Apocalypse, and in the first book of the Bible called the book of Genesis.

The End and the Beginning of scripture are the most essential parts. Genesis was written centuries before A Revelation. The last book of the Bible, A Revelation, is a prophecy, the promise given in scriptures survives, until now, when the Sovereign Seals in the original promise of God, is revealed to the world. Perhaps, the Sovereign Seals are a symbol of our salvation, our rebirth, the crowning of our consciousness, but, inevitable? The whole body of scriptures implies humanity is being put to a test. A test is a test, there is no inevitability that humanity will pass and be found or prove ourselves worthy of God's Seal.

The general theme of the scriptures are about an event that occurred after God created the world, and then, our first ancestors were added to the mix to take care of the world, constantly being manipulated by a Devil, who tricked us into failing God, who then exiled the Devil and our ancestors who continued to be tormented and tricked by the Devil. God began to formulate a plan to save us, occurring in the form of a promise and more promises along the way, that one day, Devil or no, God's Children will be saved and reclaimed by God, and the sign would coincide synchronously with the revealing of the Sovereign Seal.

When Adam and Eve tried to eat the flames of the golden lampstand, not of the tree of good and evil, they got burned and suddenly realized the light was fire, both good and evil. From then on Adam and Eve did not trust God. They feared and forgot He loved them. Love was too difficult a concept for the people to understand. The promise of God is about restoring the trust, and what better way to restore that trust then to prophesy of a day many generations away when the seal of that trust becomes restored, so promised God to the prophets.

God's promise was spoken of for generations and then eventually written down in the form of the scriptures which speak of the promise He gave our first ancestors, that someday we would understand and all the prophesy and all the people from generation to generation could read what the scriptures spoke before the Sovereign Seal could be restored to us, as the end, of what went wrong in the beginning. The terror of eating the wrong fruit, fire, from a tree of lights tempered Adam and Eve with doubt, which they passed down to their children, and was like a deadly curse, for soon no one trusted anyone.

From the moment God made His promise, the plan only proceeded a few steps. The Sovereign Seals of God and Goddess Part One is the next step on the stairway to Heaven. We are on the fourth step, 'Fa', for future generations, and with enough soul can get to the land of, 'La-Te-Da'. Remember how we got there, how we found our way back into God's good graces again, so we can pass the fulfillment of God's Promise on to future generations in a way more palatable than fire.

All of the commissions from God were always centered on a promise. In the Holy Scriptures there are more than a few promises, but most seem centered around the promise of Genesis 22:16-18. However, there is more to God's promise than meets the eye. The Children of God shall multiply like the stars of the heavens and like the grains of sand on the seashore, but in A Revelation, only 144,000 seem to be chosen to tend to the affairs of the kingdom of the New Jerusalem.

The book of A Revelation is about the last days, the end times, the fulfilment of a promise, a covenant, a sacred trust between God and our common ancestors, who invented our inherited theological jurisdictional concept of ancestry, civilization and self, as all equally family of the Most High God and Goddess. The end or resulting reason for this body of words and works is to reveal us as the 'Sovereign' people, or family, children of the Most High God and Goddess, that have a living will, or a deed of a living trust in us, Their Children.

This is a book about what is commonly called "The Scroll of the Seven Seals" that modern doomsayer Christians think heralds the end of the world and the beginning of another New Jerusalem. The Scroll of the Seven Seals is also called "The Sovereign Seal of the Most High God" and was unavailable to the human race until recently because no one had ever drawn the Sovereign Seal and lived to share it.

Anyone learned of theology from which civilization derives its culture, law, traditions, aspirations and inspirations, has read scriptures or heard of them, and among those scriptures two books predominate the focus that the world was conceived and created in the book of Genesis and how the world ends, with the last days and the end times in the book of A Revelation to John, also called the Apocalypse of John. How the world began and how it will end, where we came from and where we are going are the two predominate topics of spiritual questioning.

Both the beginning and the end, the Alpha and Omega, of scripture, Genesis and the Apocalypse, are the source of material revealing the Sovereign Seal of God which is the centerpiece of God's Plan, our symbolic end or salvation through God, the prophets, and the deliverer of the Seal, Jesus Christ. There is an implied salvation, a great and final truth once revealed, if recognized, brings to us a proof of God and a proof of Goddess, all resulting in a miraculous salvation of our people, and our world, through Our Common Mother and Father, providing the people a peaceful spirit because The Scroll of the Seven Seals validates the faith of Jesus Christ, his Apostles, and the prophets who came before, and the Sovereign Seal proves we are God's Children, His Family.

Two thousand years later, the Revelation, an Apocalypse of John, has driven the world to extremes of madness. People want the fulfillment of the prophesy in the book of A Revelation. The prophesy speaks of the kingdom of heaven becoming manifest after many trials and tribulations, and speaks of the fulfilment of God's Promise, going all of the way to the first people who told the stories thousands of years before they were written, called the Holy Scriptures, which assisted in the forming of the spiritual mindset of the religious who have formed the current body or corpus of laws.

Yes, thousands of years have passed and we are still trying to get a clue as to what the Holy Scriptures and the very scary book of A Revelation are all about. Largely, most of us think, the Apocalypse is about the end of the world, a battle between God's children and the Devil, over the possession of the world and the souls of the people.

This book's purpose is to declare victory over the Devil which few ever really could fathom. If the people accept, I offer them proof the Devil has been defeated, by presenting to them the Sovereign Seal of God and the Sovereign Seal of Goddess. Though the damage done by the Devil, nobody can fathom, is great, and the people are poised to self-destruct, God always willed that His Children have proof that they really do live in His Kingdom, the Kingdom of Heaven.

The word apocalypse means to unveil, like a masterpiece, or a wedding bride. You can kiss the bride, but never has anyone said you have to Apocalypse her, to lift the veil, to see the bride's beautiful face. The word Apocalypse is one of the most beautiful words and yet we have traditionally taken it to mean the horrible end of the world.

God is the groom and Goddess the bride, but She metaphorically becomes the holy city of the New Jerusalem, coming down from the sky. God has a vision of the future of His children, a vision about their conflicts with each other, and conflict with several enemies common to all people of the Earth, enemies that may not even have been originally indigenous to Earth. God shared His vision with His Angel, who shared God's vision with Jesus Christ, who shared it with his angel who gave the vision to John to give to the seven churches in the district of Asia, and in turn gave the vision to us because of its great import to the fulfilment of the promise of God to previous generations and for the sake of future generations. The word Asia comes from the name of a great prophet who spoke of the battle between the forces of good and evil.

Mother Goddess and Father God's feelings and thoughts are to be respected, revered but not feared, and to be loved by all dwelling on Earth and throughout Creation. Modern man is almost entirely completely opposite of what Mother Nature and Father Time were expecting. Surprise! Modern man is almost completely ignorant of God and Nature, the most miraculous beings of all, loving creation, being creation, that all beings exist because of. If modern man is told that something is "Holy", he might think of it as something that is not worth his time, because his time is too holy for such consideration for something other than himself and what he is doing. Anything worthy of the people's attention, addressed in Christian religion and other religious movements was sat upon by those trying to possess the people, their minds, hearts, bodies, souls, ideologies, the land, oceans, seas and the air you breath.

The Rule of Law, Love, and Life cannot be honored legally without the Sovereign Seals of Our Common Mother and Father being applied, in spirit, and in reality. From the Holy Scriptures we can gather that God has a Seal of Sovereignty common to the living spirits of Heaven. Passing the seals down to a living body of Earth has proven to be almost impossible. Sovereignty means jurisdictional rule of law by law, but when we think of God's Sovereignty we consider God's jurisdiction as a mere cosmic rule, a universal law, not expressed in words heard or represented as a living truth that reveals God's strength, a Divine Order, Fatherly Love, God's goodness, mathematical perfection, and all of the virtues.

Certainly, no human claim of sovereignty or symbol for the incorporation of law, no sigil, no other seal, or stamp of approval can surpass the Sovereign Seal of God, and our equality which is expressly symbolized in the Seal revealing His love for us all. If the laws of men are not harmonious with the virtues expressed in the Sovereign Seal, and do not reflect the image of God, expressed in us, then these laws should not be written, applied or enforced upon the people of God who live upon the Earth, by any other people who live upon the Earth, who might refuse God His courtesy, knowing that Earth exists in Heaven.

Our cosmic parents gave us life on Earth which exists in the Jurisdiction of the Kingdom of Heaven. Why are Their Seals of Sovereignty not on any of the founding documents of any nation, or religion? We are in the State of Unknowing. How can and should we honor our Common Cosmic Parental Units, with our lives if necessary? Scriptures have warned us about the times of tribulation, the same tribulation that inspired the Word of God, the scriptures. The quest for the Sovereign Seals is a true trial, a test of our faith, belief and love for our Creator, a test like Job's, of our individual worthiness not just our collective self-worth. Who is worthy?

There is a paradigm shift of thinking when men are supposed to be "gods", who see themselves as God's sons and daughters, the Children of God. In order to achieve this paradigm shift in our thinking, our perception of self, God sent O Immanuel, supposedly His only begotten son. At first, maybe God pulled back from teaching us everything. We suffered, what seemed like God's abandonment, from Genesis right on through the scriptures, but, in the last book, A Revelation, because of the actions of Jesus and others, God changed His mind, awarding the Seal of God to Jesus for his worthiness, who passed God's Seal on in the mystery of A Revelation. God put us to a test of worthiness which sounds more like the devil if you asked Job, and the result, if successful, would be the recognition of exactly what we are talking about, the sovereignty of the Most High, and our earning the Sovereign Seal as God's people, His children, who just returned home to heaven, paradise, from a long hard crazy hellish journey, lost, on Earth.

In the land of Uz lived Job, according to Chapter 1, verse 2, he had, "Seven sons and three daughters…" and in verse 3, "… seven thousand sheep…"; "and that man came to be the greatest of all the Orientals." In Chapter 2 verse 6, Job tells us that "It came to be the day when the sons of the true God entered to take their station before JHVH, and even Satan entered right among them. 7 And JHVH said to Satan: 'Where do you come from?' At that Satan answered JHVH and said, 'From roving about in the earth and walking about in it.'" God does not know who Satan is and yet knows that he is there to "set" his heart upon God's servant Job. 8 "There is no one like him in the earth", a man blameless and upright, fearing God and turning aside from bad." I am sure none of us knows what is going on here in the book of Job, and that either God is insanely forgetful and yet still fore-knowing or the text is miswritten. We have very few scriptures that tell us about Set, or Satan, who is always changing appearance, a shapeshifter capable of perhaps deceiving even JHVH, God. What chance do we have in our relatively short lives to make good or even have some sense that our history and our lives as a people have been misled and corrupted by a trickster capable of bringing us all to ruin, and there is little if anything at all that we can do about it?

Job. Chapter 2, verse 1 through 9 puts the reader in Job's shoes, because Job's shoes are our shoes. Even when doing everything right, Job, after experiencing such horror and misfortune, said to his wife in verse 9, "Shall we accept merely what is good from the true God and not accept also what is bad?"

Only those with a good impression from the Holy Scriptures, related to the actions of God, have even the slightest notion that there may have been a war. From the scriptures, the only way that we will know that the war is over is when the Sovereign Seal is revealed. There have been many great thinkers, philosophers, mathematicians, scientists, like Lao Tzu, Confucius, Archimedes, Pythagoras, Aristotle, Plato, Leonardo DaVinci, Sir Isaac Newton, Einstein, Nicola Tesla and more that have revolutionized and pioneered their field of study; and yet no one in the history of humanity ever discovered the Sacred Seal of God.

The story says, God had a plan for our salvation for a long, long time. But that story contains the most unbelievable catch, there were some alien-looking beings denying God His plan for our salvation from coming to fruition, right from the start of our being created. The idea that none of our ancestors, who have inhabited the Earth for millions of years, had discovered the Sovereign Seals leads me to believe there was an intentional act, by some extra-terrestrial beings, to conceal the true identity of God, our knowledge of God and deny us our divinity. When I say extra-terrestrial, I am thinking about aliens in spaceships, "overlords". Why would extra-terrestrials conceal and deny us our common divinity? The Sovereign Seals fit the bill for what would most quickly assist Goddess and God for the rapid perfecting of our own individual reasoning and collective being; and certainly seems to be just the kind of thing, the very thing, that our 'God' and our 'Goddess' would want and need us to have, to be who and what They need us to be, in communion with Them.

Many early civilizations of humanity's past have a very similar story in what is left of their collective histories, which is why there are so many names in their histories and myths for only a few beings with extraordinarily different, alien-looking features. Our early civilizations recurrently collapsed when extra-terrestrial beings, 'gods', showed up. They attacked where people were finding the truths in all things, the language of creation through the mandala teaching and the study of the world through sacred geometry and sacred measure, where the centers of civilization and higher learning were constructed with a knowledge of sacred geometry. The evil ones, 'gods', killed the philosophers, astronomers, mathematicians, scientists, knowledge of the Sacred Goddess, God and as many free-thinking men and women as possible. In the wake of the assault of the evil ones upon humanity, entire civilizations of humanity's earliest histories have been nearly lost, before the fruits of their labor could come to flower.

Our enlightenment drew attacks from these 'other', non-human looking beings, who had in their arsenal the ability to copy a person's image, and fake out those who know the person's appearance into thinking the person is who they appear to be, when in fact the person is an extra-terrestrial, the vile evil ones as depicted in the Holy Scripture, and etched in stone and glyph of humanity's earliest histories. One such deception, or mimic, brought the 'fall' of mankind, from the grace of the host of the garden of Eden, a deception by a reptilian, snake, serpent, cherubin, seraphim, dragon, naga, jinn or djinn, Oni, Asuras, Durgas, devil, fallen angel, demon, Oomay, person or persons, both 'sexes' with at least one 'female' and a 'male' are some of the names given those who toppled the efforts of our ancestors throughout the world working for our future enlightenment. We spoke one tongue, one language, and the evil ones scattered us and confused our tongues. The book of Genesis tells us so.

Christ left us with few words, warning us of certain beings ruining everything our God deemed as humanity's inheritance that we were to receive through Jesus Christ. The gospels tell us enough, everything was at stake. Afterwards, the Revelation was given to the Apostle John. Then after the resurrection, at the Pentecost, people again spoke the same language, that of the Holy Ghost.

How was Jesus aware of these beings with the frontal lobe projections called horns? The horned ones could have been on him from the start. In fact, the prophecies only served to reveal Jesus, to point him out before he came to be, informing mankind, and those who were not mankind about the arrival of Jesus. Though the people in general had confusing beliefs about these 'beings', the evil ones, Jesus seemed to have had personal experiences in which he was at arm's length from the Devil. Jesus gave his testimony as to the authenticity of the event. No one else happened to be there when Jesus and the Devil had words, but God was watching. The events that unfolded in the desert when Jesus met the Devil were about the establishment of God's kingdom on Earth.

These evil beings working against God's will have been controlling human fate and destiny as long as history records. Once born we are given foresight, maybe even before birth? Our foresight wrestles with our afterthoughts until a moment of destiny pits God's will against fates that are meant to be overcome. God has refused to give up hope to fate and chance and is revealing the kingdom of God. With the Sovereign Seal upon the Earth, the Seal of the God of Heaven revealed, the remainder of the evil ones and those who were once possessed by them, are no longer a threat to the children of Goddess and God.

No body but God and Goddess could have seen everything and guided the prophets and others, who guided the children of God, to gratefully overcome and defeat the evil ones, who were so few, but could turn so many of us against each other. The revelation does not mean that man is worthy. Mankind is unworthy. He is a huge monstrous mess. Historically speaking, mankind has failed in all things that God requests, and is on the verge of self-annihilation, ecological suicide, eco-genocide. However, mankind has been freed from the clutches of the evil ones only a short time ago and now for a brief, or perhaps an enduring moment, we the people can reclaim our divinity and our sovereignty as the Children of God living in Heaven on Earth. If mankind would have had the Sovereign Seal a long time ago he would have not seen himself as mankind but godkind.

The Sovereign Seal is the centerpiece of the scariest book in the Holy Scriptures, the Apocalypse, the Revelation to John, the last book, about the last days, which describes a battle, a war, the scriptures in a nutshell, still raging in the end times, though the war began long, long ago, in the beginning times. Are we talking, millions of years?

Rule by the threat of death, pain and torture for those who question the rules lost its efficacy a long time ago when our lives became shortened, the environment degraded, and love, like that of the sweet Lord, Jesus, who both loved life and did not fear death, bucked every trend of the evil empire, for he knew that we have been living in the paradox of the anti-paradise paradigm. The evil empire has come to an end, for the revelation of the Sovereign Seal is with us, in our hands, and is the paragon itself, the very pattern par excellence which restores the soul to the thesis for which we were created, as Jesus proclaimed in his Sermon on the Mount, to a state of supreme happiness, which is a state of perfection, that cannot be taken away from us by those who love not life, but themselves, who seek to control without consent.

Our entire history is the history of war. Before that, there must have been territorial disputes, like children fighting over a toy. Over time these disputes have turned into periods of mass reciprocal destruction. Laying on the battlefield of war, somebody's loved ones die. Maybe the Sovereign Seal can bring us back home from the battle and help us regain our sense of sanity? I hope so!

There are those who think they have sovereignty over us, our souls, minds, hearts and bodies as slaves not as a free-thinking people. Our money, votes, land and children all belong to those who have claimed sovereignty over us and claim to be our master while they fail to understand anything real about being a spiritual being.

God Almighty gave you your father and your mother to be yours. All will fight to take over that fragile heart, that infinite mind of yours, and force you to serve them first, not God first, which should be the primary impetus behind every willful act of a responsible being. And before you can serve anyone for anything, remember, choice requires your mind being free first that your independent volition have any actuality.

Scripture implores that our lives, our history, the histories of all of our ancestors were always in a war for our souls, a war, between God and well, not God. The prophesies, the good ones, speak to the people of the later times, the fight for salvation. In these times and future times, the people are faced with a final choice, and their eternal souls are all caught up in the bargain. The choice is as follows: either become a part of the Kingdom of Heaven, both above and below, and behave like good children of God and Goddess, with grace, or suffer the many and the final consequences.

If the people choose the path leading to destruction, every consequence will make life more unlivable, unbearable, more insane and horrible, which makes the idea that reality is God's world more unbelievable. Of course, the adoption of the Sovereign Seals as living proof of the path of salvation and life will bear the opposite results. The choice is obvious, the hour is late.

In order for a new path, world and perception of self to take root and flourish we need to realize the signature in the deed of trust in doing God's work, reading and understanding the contract. Then, we need the Seal of God for approval.

Our world, Earth in Heaven, is a place full of miraculous qualities and is sacred to God. John 3:16, "For God so loved the world, he sent His Son in order that everyone exercising faith in Him might not be destroyed but have everlasting life." That was over two thousand years ago. We were already so far away from the path of life and salvation then, that God sent His Son.

Jesus had been prepared for any outcome, knowing that he had what he needed to found and establish the Kingdom of Heaven upon the Earth, for God, Earth, and its inhabitants, whom Goddess and God consider Their Children. The Sovereign Seal must have been in His mind along with a layout, a blueprint for the New Jerusalem.

However, Jesus was unnecessarily crucified instead of being received as the King, and so, the inhabitants of Earth did not inherit the Kingdom of Heaven as God promised in applicable prophecies. So, what happened? The people inherited Hell on Earth instead. This book on the Scroll of the Sovereign Seals offers the people of Earth certain special proofs, promised to us by God, which Jesus and his apostles left behind in the documents contained in the Holy Scriptures.

Since the invention of the printing press, those documents were provided to many, many people, all around the world. Even today people draw spiritual inspiration from these documents which are found in Hebrew traditions, Christianity, Islam, and many other ancient texts, like some of the Gnostic texts of early Coptic Christians in Egypt.

You may not know now what God has planned for the people of the Earth. You are a person of Earth and what you believe you are, is in every breath you take. What you learn in life will impact your perception of self, every cell in your body, and those around you, your friends, neighbors, relatives, and co-inhabitants of our home, Earth.

If you are human, you may sense that the end is near, and closing in on the people of Earth. The feelings of doom and dread can shake a man, a people, and keep shaking them, until, if ever they regain their senses, and return to the path. The peoples of the world are in turmoil. Their chance to be of one spiritual mind is at hand. Will the end times, the last days, be the end, the end of mankind, the world, hell on Earth, or the end for those searching for the long-awaited proof of God and Goddess?

Jesus said one last chance should be administered to mankind so that all of mankind shall clearly see, they are godkind. The prophesies point to the end times as the last chance, the final and perhaps best chance, given to the people to see themselves, as the people of Earth, reclaim their divinity, and bring an end to the corruption ruining life for current and future generations. Long ago, the patriarchs of ages past were promised that the people of Earth would receive the Sovereign Seal. Looking for evidence of the Seal's existence was challenging. I tried and found only a little evidence. However, I did find a recurring theme of a power struggle between beings who wanted mankind to have the Sovereign Seal and beings who did not.

In the end, the Sovereign Seal is with us. There is no evidence anywhere on Earth that the Sovereign Seal was ever real. We might not have known about the Sovereign Seal if not for Jesus Christ giving John the prophesy called a Revelation to John, or the Apocalypse, in which the pieces and the story about the Sovereign Seal of the Most High God are described in mysterious, shocking, eye-opening ways. The fact that only now the Sovereign Seal is "real" to us and can be witnessed and validated by us through scripture, is shocking to me.

Everything would be better if we understood that the only correct thing to do to return to paradise is honor the sacred trust placed in us, to stop harming the world, all the living things upon the Earth have a right to be here too, and mankind violates the sacred trust of the living things by destroying the world's ecosystems, driving species to extinction. We must protect the world from us. We are the ones causing all of the harm. We must protect the world from those causing harm to the world, and that being us, we must stop ourselves and those amongst us from causing harm to the world. Stopping the destructive behavior of humanity is of paramount importance because we all suffer the consequences. How are we to stop ourselves and others from doing harm, without being hurt by those willing to hurt us to continue destroying the world? From the oldest times the use of the threat of death controlled civilization, which, by the way, was the key of the empire. The after-life is looking at what we did and did not do.

We need a genuine spiritual perception of self that explains how we are divine, to assist us in the work of taking good care of Great Nature. All that I can offer, that Our Heavenly Mother and Father were not able to get across the threshold, are the Sovereign Seals, which was offered up to the one who was worthy, to unveil the Scroll of the Sevens Seals, which now by the grace of God, the Lord Jesus Christ, and others, has crossed the threshold into our hands, hearts, and our homes. I confess, I have seen so much beauty that cannot be weighed, measured, bought, sold, or treasured, because beauty is everywhere; but, when I saw the Sovereign Seals of the Most High for the first time its beauty saturated my soul, with what I can only guess is the Holy Spirit. I can only hope, as I hope God and Goddess hope, that the revelation of the Sovereign Seals will "deliver us from evil." I did not have an instant full paradigm shift, but, as I studied everything I could find relative to the Sovereign Seals, the more I sensed them messaging me, saying, "You are a god." The perception of myself as a god put me into conflict with all of the notions that I learned; that I was certainly not a god, but a poor man, a broken man. The Sovereign Seals just repeated their message, "You are a god." But I am too humble, modest, and frail I thought. The Seals spoke directly to my old weary heart and soul, which then began to feel young and perhaps like an eternal soul is supposed to feel.

My hope is that The Sovereign Seals facilitates a similar grace for others. For now, as I stroll through the old city where freedom's banner yet waves, I solemnly give thanks for those who fought for our freedom, for those brave souls who fought for a life they believed in, and I must believe in too, that we each have our own individual sovereign rights. We each have sovereignty over our own spirit and soul which no one on Earth can place a real claim on.

✯ <u>The Sovereign Seals</u> ✯

There is a story that has been five thousand years or more in the making. Scripture set the stage for Jesus Christ and he set the stage for this book. The History of Seals is not just about sealing wax and other fancy stuff. Seals are about the very idea of kingdom and kingship. Our individual sovereignty, proof of God and Goddess, Their Sovereign Seals, is what we have been fighting for over thousands of years of struggle to set free, a truth buried like a treasure.

Cylinder Seals originated in Mesopotamia, in Babylon, and are being dated back through the fourth millennium B.C. The Chalcolithic Age (Copper Age), and Aeneolithic Age (Bronze Age) seal impressions go all the way back to a very early unknown pictographic script. Edith Porada, an expert in cylinder seals, says the bejeweled seals were rubbed with oil before being rolled with the fingers to make an impression in clay. The oil was to keep the clay from sticking to the seal and ruining the impression. Assyrian and Egyptian cylinders had a wire threaded through the center of the cylinder to roll out the impression.

Earlier Egyptian seals were made of carved wood, baked clay, and some soft stones. These were used for a few thousand years until the stamp types began around 700 B.C. The Hittites and Palestinians had been using the preferred stamp type seal that came out of Mesopotamia sometime quite earlier.

Cylinder Seals are carved in reverse, a mirror image, and powder was ground into the image to finish a seal. Bow-drills were used to bore through the length of the seal. Seal-cutters used sharp instruments, chisels of copper, and whetstones were used in the craft of the making of these cylinder seals.

Sealing became so important that guilds of sealers were taught and maintained to handle the large load of work in commodities for shipment. Wine, olive oil and linens, luxury items and bales of goods, were all sealed. The book of Job mentions a sealed bag, (14:17), and (38:14) speaks that the natural world turns to God as "clay to the seal".

Seals were used when security and purity was important. So, with a jar of wine a stopper was placed in the mouth tied in place with cord or linen bandings, which was then covered with a lump of clay. Over that an inspector's seal is stamped or rolled with a cylinder seal. Then, a blob of plaster capped the top and that was pressed with the royal seal.

The use of seals is throughout scriptures and goes all of the way back to the handprints left painted in 30,000-year-old cave art. If you suppose yourself the artist, how would you have left your mark, your print, your signature in a cave 30,000 years ago? The handprints speak, "I am. I am the artist who drew and painted these things." With that in mind think of all those who say, "I am" with identifiable marks, names, family crests, sigils, banners, colors, addresses, phone numbers, identity numbers.

Making your mark goes to the roots of people's perception of self, evolving. Is marking something as yours an organic expression of the ego, true ego or false ego? Where civilization first used sealing, with implements called seals, or sigils, meaning symbolic signatures also called seals, clay and wax were used to print or imprint, copy, or duplicate the impression, by pressing it, literally the first printing presses, is what the seals were.

Archeological excavations in the Near East have found tens of thousands of tiny seals in Mesopotamia alone. One cannot overstate the importance of seals in those cultures. Imagine the time of Hammurabi the lawgiver, the 18th century B.C. or earlier king of Babylon. And then think back much farther. The large collections of these seals allowed scholars to track their evolution back to the sites at Uruk, to a period of over five thousand years ago, or 3,200 B.C. The long-lasting fad of the use of these implements for identification was fizzling out in Persian Palestine about 300 B.C.

Mesopotamian seals are called the cylinder seal type. They are like a spool about the size of thimbles or a finger bone. These were also probably used more for carpet weavers in Persia who preferred a more conical design, though much earlier in Mesopotamia the spools were longer, and they were like Faberge Eggs in that they were fancier with engravings of religious scenes and symbols. Other things depicted were animals, trades, customs, clothing. Button stamp seals, Persian conical seals, and cylinder seals are the three main types. Some depict mythic scenes of the gods and goddesses. Some have intricate brocade patterns.

Seal Makers, the engravers, were highly prized for their knowledge of glyphs and were spared from battle and spared after a battle. The primary use of seals was to affix the equivalent of a signature for royal or religious documents. In Mesopotamia when statements had been printed with a stylus to write in cuneiform on wet clay tablets, the scribe called for witnesses and the negotiator's personal cylinder seals were rolled over on the tablet legalizing the contract.

Mesopotamian cylinder seals sometimes depicted the buyers, sellers, senders, and receivers, revealing commercial contracting in its earliest forms. Coins and currencies have similar histories.

The Sovereign Seal is a mystery from the start because there has always been the idea of the wonderful creature, the seal, but there has not always been the idea of an 'engraved' seal, a symbol, sealing the deal of a covenant between God, and 'man', Moses and the sons of Israel. Did the skin of a seal inspire the idea of a Sovereign Seal? A Seal keeps things preserved, dry, shields, and saves that which is holy to us from getting soaked, sick, and muddy.

Many of the definitions for the word seal comes from the use of seal skins, mentioned in the book of Numbers five times, in chapter 4:6-14. The word used is 'sealskins', denoting the skins taken from seals, the amphibious mammal. Sealskins are used as a water resisting cover for the tent "of the tabernacle and all that is in it, namely, the holy place and all its utensils." This same tent is in Rev.: 15:5, "And after these things I saw, and the sanctuary of the tent of the witness was opened in heaven."

In A Revelation 10:2, there is an intentional usage of the same word having a double meaning, to bring together one idea, sovereignty, over the people, land, and sea. "And he set his right foot upon the sea, but his left one upon the earth,". The word seal has a dual meaning referencing the creature, a seal upon the shore, and the passage of a Seal. In the case of Rev. 10:2 the Scroll of the Seven Seals is passed to an angel who stands upon the shore. Again, in A Revelation 10:5, 6 and 8, the land and sea, are one. The seven thunders speak, and the words are "Sealed up". Later, in A Revelation 20:3, The Devil, Satan is seized, bound, and thrown into the abyss, and it is "sealed" over him.

The word seal can be used as a verb meaning to fasten or close tightly by or as if by a seal. Seal means to close by any form of fastening that must be broken to gain access to what is within. One's own handshake serves as one's word, one's bond, promise, confirmation, assurance, to assure, confirm or bind, and with some spit seal the deal.

Seals are a common token, particularly in the ancient Orient, of a person's property rights or power. In the Bible and in Christian literature, seals, like coins, are sometimes mentioned as a symbol of belonging to God. Divine secrets are also sealed. In the Apocalypse, the Lamb opens the scroll with seven seals.

To authorize testimony or make a marriage official it must be sealed with certification. "You may kiss the bride." Now, how to seal the deal, with a quick peck on the lips, or a full blown apoca-lips? The kiss of life, symbolized by the first kiss of marriage, is when God and Goddess first touch and the divinity of the spark of life is freed.

The word seal is applied in spirit and letters when somebody gets their confirmation, baptism, adoption papers, walking papers, licenses, or certifications to legally bind forever, for whatever commission the adjudication occasions, is what sealing wax and other fancy stuff is all about. Sealing wax is a resinous preparation that gets soft when heated and is not used for home repair, but is used for sealing documents.

Seals are applied to everyday things that involve our lives. I sent a letter the other day. The act doesn't seem like such a big deal, but it is a sealed deal, a big deal, that goes way back in time to the very idea of sovereign rights.

A seal is anything that tightly closes completely securing a thing, as in closures, fasteners for everything from doors and windows to the adhesive on an envelope or stamp or tape. So, when you send a letter, a holiday greeting card, the idea of the seal is applied repeatedly to the process. The envelope you are mailing requires a seal, the adhesive glue is a seal. When you close the envelope, and it sticks and stays closed you have sealed the seal. The stamp used to mail the letter is also a seal, and the sticky stuff stuck on the stamp is a seal. The cancellation date or post mark is a seal. The dollar used to buy the stamp has the Great Seal upon it. When your letter is opened the seal has been broken. And if you put an Easter Seal on the letter for decorative purposes, you may find extra jelly beans in your basket.

When we talk about the very essence of what a seal is, we are talking about impressions. We say, "I want to make a good impression." Why? To get the approval of someone whose approval is sought. Are you buying? Are you selling? What is your product? What is your pitch? How will you seal the deal, so they get what they want or need, and you get what you want or need? A seal is your mark, your footprint, fingerprint. Your seal is your identifying signs, your signature, something that you identify yourself through. Your voice, your song, your teeth, all you are in your own body, heart, mind, spirit, and soul expresses itself in a vehicle that is sealed or else we would all be bleeding all over the place. Have you ever received the Eucharist? Have you ever signed your name in blood? I read somewhere that John the Revelator, was in prison on Patmos Island at the time he wrote the Apocalypse, and he wrote it with his own blood. Abel's blood cried from the ground. Does John's blood cry out from the book of Revelations? Does Jesus's blood cry out from Golgatha?

So much of the idea of a seal has to do with what is called, Sacred Trust. The reason for a folded envelope implies the contents should not spill out. The adhesive bond is the sealing agent applied invoking the sacred trust in the messenger of the sealed contents, that those contents are insured to be delivered without tampering or altering from sender to the receiver, implying that what's inside the envelope is the genuine article, "the real McCoy".

A seal can be a letter, a word, a symbol, an embossed emblem that sends the message of attestation of authenticity and is an item used to imprint a seal, like a ring, or medallion engraved with the impression to be imprinted onto other sealing agents like wax, lead, and paper when the possessor of the seal applies it. Sealing was used to send legal documents formally used to impart an order from a higher court of appeals. The Queen used her signet ring, her seal, to seal the documents. The impression left is also a seal, though it is only a copy of the real royal sigil.

Both The Declaration of Independence and The Constitution are not sealed. The Declaration of Independence was signed and dated, and The Constitution was signed before receiving an adoption date, which means two things. The laws are suggestions and are not enforce-able because they are unsealed, and you don't know those people who wrote the founding documents because they are dead. There could be an explanation for why the founding documents are unsealed. That explanation hasn't been delivered yet. The Postmaster General is still waiting to hear from the Creator of endowments.

The founders were at a crossroad, in order to deny the king's sovereignty over the people as subjects, the founders had to acknowledge their own divinity, and equally the divinity in others, including God's divinity over them. Equal sovereignty for all is hard to conceive of. The catch was the founders would have to prove God exists, and could not, and therefore declared Divine Providence, without the divine Seal of God.

The most obvious thing of all is Goddess and God are Real. To say you believe, is to say you believe in Them, and doesn't really say anything more, or less, or the opposite. You have got to prove Divine Providence either way, and if you are not God or the Goddess, you cannot prove they exist. If you were God, would you have to ask yourself, "Am I God?" Why would God impose upon you, or your-self, any other supposition about His Self, like "Am I Real?" To believe or not to believe, neither really explains enough. Why? Because God is Real. How do I know? For the Sovereign Seals tell me so.

The Sovereign Seal is a sigil, the signet, the seal, the signature of Our Heavenly Father and His claim of jurisdictional Sovereignty has providence over the claims of any person or nation, their laws and claims of jurisdictional proclamations and enforcement of claims, claiming claims, over anyone or anything are false claims. I am, and all that is mine, He has possession of, giving me the freedom to disregard any and all claims any nation or person may have regarding my person, and my personal possessions, which belong to Heaven and to God and His Goddess, all through my brother, the Lord Jesus Christ. The truth that sets us free is the recognition of God's Sovereignty.

God's Seal is to be used as the sigil of the Most High God, according to the Revelation of the Last Man, to give to the gods and goddesses of the future final eternal generation, God's Children, you, forever to remind them, yourselves, that we are God's Children on Earth, which is in

Heaven; and as such, we are therefore required to recognize our place in the world as such. The Sovereign Seal is a jurisdictional judgement, a fact, of God's Will, and an inheritance of God's love, extended like open arms always receiving us. But, once revealed, disclosed, described, vocalized, and written, the people are requested and required to recognize God through His Seal. Stop what you are doing, take a deep breath and with gratitude release it. God is with you, with us all.

Given grace from the Most High, I bring the people a genuine revelation from the Most High, Who long ago gave His prophets glimpses of our day back in those days, thousands of years ago, when people sought salvation for future generations from their oppressors making jurisdictional claims, claiming possession over the land and the people like the cattle, sheep, goats and other livestock.

From Goddess and from God, I have for you, the oppressed, a revelation, that you have been lied to and deceived like your ancestors from the very beginning of our creation. Please be aware, that a revelation is the moment when something not known becomes known. May that which becomes known empower you with a God-given sense of self and being, to fight against the evil ways of evil people who claim, falsely, sovereignty or sovereign rights over others and enslave them with those evil ways, called laws, for which obedience is demanded by imprisonment or death. Is that what sovereignty really means, the right of dominion by threat of death? And dominion by rule of law by the threat of death, does that sound fair, equal, just, balanced, or cruel and insane? Shoot or be shot is not the way of Heaven.

The last day is coming. When it does arrive, there will be nothing anyone on Earth can do. Before that day comes, scripture tells us, there will be signs. The most powerful sign and powerful warning will come as a final warning to selfish evil people and good people alike in the form of a scroll from God called the "Scroll of the Seven Seals." To look upon the Scroll of the Seven Seals is to reawaken the divine spirit and the divine soul in the beholder.

God did not give man the atom bomb and detonate it upon His own Earth. No, men, who thought they were like 'gods' but, had no proof that they might be, did and called incinerating half a million people in a matter of seconds proof of their godliness. Man has become more and more evil with each passing generation, such that the Devil might concur with God for once on the complete insanity of man and cry out, "Do something God! They have gone too far!"

Evil must cease, one way or another, the evil of men will cease. Those who have had near death experiences will occasionally comment that when an evil person dies their spirit and soul is dealt with by the innocent people harmed by the evil person. There, among the dead, every day is Judgement Day.

Religion is suppose to be 'the way', but no matter which way you turn, there's a trap, or your way is blocked, but, God and Goddess, and the goodness of creation is everywhere, unless, of course, you are a teenager, sitting in school, directly across from the person that you have a crush on, and the zit on your cheek is fit to burst, everyone is looking, wondering, when they may have to duck. Maybe such embarrassing moments makes a person become an Atheist, because after something like that, of course proof of God is required. You want proof because there are unbelievable experiences and facts we witness constantly from within our frail mortal earthen bodies.

The book of Job is a well written ancient appraisal of the 'human' condition. Such was Job's life that if he were to deny God, Job's denial would have been justifiable. But rather than live in disbelief and anguish, Job lived in belief and anguish. We are Job and do not have to suffer the 'human' condition. We can change. In the story of Job there is a God, devil, and a lot of witnesses as to the more horrific aspects of our divine existence.

I think when people say they do not believe in God that the opposite is true. Life is so destructive and painful that people get shell-shocked into a state of general disbelief because they are afraid that the world has lost its mind, like Job could have after all of the evil he suffered.

You are Job. We are Job. We can be just as faithful and God-fearing and God-loving as Job or Jesus, and still, sure as you were born you will die, and sure as we are born, we die. Life seems unfair, unjust. Yet, without death there is no life, and without life there is no death. You do not want to destroy the world because you are going to die, do you? Maybe therein lies the real truth, we love life too much.

I am sorry that life and death, existence, seems like a pathetic display of constant insanity by insane archetypes hammering humans into mortar to patch a crack between Heaven and Hell. We ask God why? What we do not know may explain everything.

There is too much responsibility for any individual to be singled out as the leader or leaders, controlling the thoughts, feelings, and lives of others. Surrendering one's own individual sovereignty is highly irresponsible for any responsible being.

Individual sovereignty is the first and last rite though we have no proven choice in being born or in dying. God's Sovereignty allows us the hope in individual sovereignty relative to our place in our civilization. Do the people derive individual sovereignty or national sovereignty as bestowed upon them by God, "Opus Dei", or from Great Nature, or from unsealed declarative self or group proscriptions?

The Sovereign Seals are to be celebrated, talked about, and shared. Share the Seal of God and Goddess for Their Seals of approval are here. Heaven is on Earth. Sovereignty is a claim of Jurisdiction and ownership of all that exists within the claimed domain. The Sovereign Seal of God means, He is claiming His kingdom. The many great nations of the world have claimed jurisdiction over you and the land. No one, not even a nation can own you or the land. The opposite has more truth in that we bury our dead. The land claims our deceased bodies as we decompose into the dirt from which God created us. Liberty is defined as the freedom to go where and do as one chooses and pleases. God gave you that freedom. How you choose to live is your right as a child of God.

No longer can the Children of God tolerate evil if we are to establish the Kingdom of Heaven on Earth. Christ teaches us to carry our own cross. We are responsible for our own salvation. Humanity can either live in Hell on Earth or Heaven on Earth. The claims to land and enforcement of policies has made slaves of God's Children. You are God's children, capable of deciding for yourself what's best. God gave you that ability. So celebrate your God given freedom. Rejoice! for I am about to reveal the Sacred Secret, the Sovereign Seals of God and Goddess.

Symbolism is a major component of religious faiths and beliefs. Where the cross in the crucifixion has several meanings, the plaque, hammered into the ground, identifying the spot where Jesus was crucified, called him the "King of Jews." In Matthew 27:27-30, Jesus received his crown, the crown of thorns, like God's Glory, is the Sovereign Seal of God. The cruel sarcastic act of crowning Jesus with the crown of thorns fulfilled prophesy.

Remember, you are free, to think for yourself. The laws, rules, morals, beliefs, creeds, and constitutions declare that freedom is real, a choice, equality under the rule of law, and the Rule of God, and in order to keep seeking the truth and live responsibly, we must be free to do so. Remember, Jesus encouraged us to seek the truth. Ask and you shall receive. Seek and you shall find. Knock and all doors will open before you. Doubt has nothing to do with seeking truth, but with weighing it for fairness. We must be free to pursue truth, for we are asked by the Lord to do so, for in the truth new freedom might be realized, a new knowledge observed.

You, the children of God the Father and the Mother Goddess do not belong to and can not be owned by, any organized religions, governments, banks or anyone else who claims ownership of you. Remember all of the great many living things, the people, the world, the land, air, water, oceans and mountains do not belong to anyone.

Currently, all governments of the world are essentially making false claims of national, local, or international sovereignty. Real jurisdictional sovereignty is to make a claim, a statement of ownership, but who takes a bowel movement and plants a flag in it? The world we live in belongs to God, everyone, and no one. God wills that each person be free in His eyes, equal in His eyes as His own Children. However, God is also Law, the rule of law, and the spirit of the law is an extension of His will. God's will should retain the only standard observed, respective of Earth and all of the beings of Earth, as it is in Heaven.

Ephesians 1:13, "But you also hoped in him after you heard the word of truth, the good news about your salvation. After you believed you were sealed by means of him with the promised holy spirit," Acts 1:7, "He said to them: "It does not belong to you to get knowledge of the times or seasons which the Father has placed in his own jurisdiction;""

From the last two verses of Matthew we hear Jesus make a huge claim that sums up what Christians would call Jesus Christ's Sovereignty claimed by Jesus throughout the Gospels and the New Testament. Mat.: 28:18-19. "18 And Jesus approached and spoke to them, saying: "All authority has been given me in heaven and on earth. 19 Go therefore and make disciples of people of all the nations, baptizing them in the name of the Father and of the Son and of the holy spirit, 20 teaching them to observe all the things I have commanded you. And, look! I am with you all the days until the conclusion of the system of things.""

What is sovereignty? Is it jurisdictional dominion? Yes. In the beginning God had so much jurisdiction, dominion over the world that when He spoke the world responded by doing what He said. When God told Adam not to do something God's jurisdictional dominion was questioned. Everything else was doing what it was told to do. And then, paradise was corrupted, so to speak, when a talking serpent with a forked tongue questioned God's dominion and brought ruin, through our first ancestors, into the world?

Is sovereignty just dominion over certain beliefs related to only certain essential and chosen rights? Sovereign rights are called freedoms, and the freedom to speak must be one, or else creation would still be waiting around to hear God's word. No one has dominion over God's Sovereignty, but if man cannot hear God, how is man supposed to obey or disobey? We have some self-sovereignty, but our self-sovereignty is nullified when a nation and people enforce the laws that take our self-sovereignty away.

Yes, we may have freedom of choice, but our freedom to choose is only for a limited time and place. Do individuals have sovereignty over the nations or do the nations have sovereignty over the individuals and their common claims to the same stuff?

The core truth can only be realized by a simple and obvious principle of the absolute ensovereignizing equity of law and justice for all, without the common cosmic ties we all share being excluded. For instance, the Inca and the Dinka may be such distant cousins, that they forgot each other even existed. But that is okay, because we are one people anyway.

Sovereign citizenry is only stable, balanced, just, and fair, when built upon the principle of equality. The principle of equality is the only spiritually expressed reality that conforms to nature. When a principle is established into law for the establishment of spiritual governance that established law influences the people to see that principle at work in themselves as civilization develops over time.

The Sovereign Seal defines for the "human" race the spiritual lawful essence that the Most High compels objectively and subjectively throughout creation and within the beings themselves, the sense of sovereignty, the sense of God's Sovereignty and our individual sense of sovereignty. As a living deed of trust the Sovereign Seal is a spiritual revelation of Law of the Living God, Great Nature, mathematics, geometry and cosmic law, that pre-exists us and our soul's journey to and from this world.

In Sanskrit, scrolling letters for words, documents, and laws, was considered sacred and holy, the act of drawing them, scribing them, made them scripture. Does your birth certificate, mortgage, or social security number look like scripture, sacred and holy? Do your documents incorporate you into the kingdom of God and Goddess or make you susceptible to the abuses of corporate lawyers of the great lie, proclaiming sovereignty over you.

Compulsories from the Goddess and God are involuntarily experienced by the messenger, but others may view the declaration as voluntary, chosen personally. Moses comes to mind as another who had doubts about being able to do what he was being compelled to do, and even called himself, God's slave. In a special revelation, all are to be notified, required to recognize the revelation, and comply with the declaratives. Even for those who cannot reason for themselves compliance is required to save them from whatever consequence might befall the disobedient.

Lot was ordered to escape the District of Sodom and Gomorrah and told not to look back. When his wife looked back upon the destruction the consequence was unfortunate for the woman was turned into a pillar of salt, Genesis 19:26. Such is scripture, even Adam and Eve failed to comply with God's directive and the result got them exiled from the Garden of Eden.

The disclosure of the Sovereign Seal is a special revelation to all people of all nations, tribes, kingdoms, religions, schools of learning, and other non-governmental organizations, including those who are not yet able to reason responsibly like a 'goddess' or 'god' might be able to do or be. The Sovereign Seal, legally, spiritually and jurisdictionally, places a deed of claim of action upon the people of the Earth, which is in Heaven, serving as a proof for the assertion of God's and Goddess's Sovereignty over the actions and affairs of the people, who are reminded by this disclosure that they are in fact, the children of the Most High.

All laws are contracts, which should be read aloud, written, some sworn by an oath routinely, and questioned routinely that The Most High, namely Goddess and God are honored first. Then laws and contracts are signed, dated, and sealed, with the varied subsequent seals, and finally, sealed with the Sovereign Seals of Goddess and God. The action of sealing our laws with the Sovereign Seals brings the assumption of divine mandates for which the implication is made for the considerations, blessings or punishments from the people on the people. We are tiny bits of a great Heaven, not the whole of it. Thus, there are mandates on the people as individuals and as groups of individuals. Compliance with Goddess and God's wishes engenders us to become grateful, pleased to assist and apologetic.

The prophets call these times the end times because the world of man is no more, man is no longer man, for to witness, to view, and to see the Sovereign Seals, by the species of law has the forbearance of the redemptive, redeeming quality of a baptism by holy spirit, which means all previous contracts, all contracts without the Seals, are technically null and void, as you would expect, because mankind is no more and the contracts and constitutions were all written, without God's or Goddess's permission, consent or proof. Unsealed documents do not require obedience.

What we have, therefore, is a new perception of self, a rebirth, requiring the rewording of those previous contracts, many, most of which would reveal how laws without the considerations, of great Mother Nature, and Her God being given due providence, are evil. The people have become evil as a result of the claims of unproven divine providence by self-centered evil Mammonites claiming powers to rule, which they have never ever had.

No one can rule over the lives of people or the world, because when you let them rule over you, you will not acquire the conscience required by the Most High to endure life or the afterlife. Freedom of will is essential, in Heaven and on Earth.

Originally, the sacraments of religions were utilized for the new initiates and practitioners attempt to make a connection to the ancestors who lead to the God and Goddess, makers, progenitors, procreators of creation.

The spiritual law associated with the Sovereign Seal carries the greatest gravity as a legally spiritualized activation device designating the will, approval or disapproval, of God and Goddess in the affairs of Heaven.

Recognizing the spiritual law associated with the Sovereign Seals connects through us to Earth, making the Kingdom of Heaven extend to the people of Earth, as equal sovereigns in the caretaking of the Earth, and all that is on Earth sharing common dominion.

Not even the Popes or anyone else among the living can solely be the bearer of the Sovereign Seal. Even Jesus was not 'alive' supposedly when the scroll was revealed to John, who wrote, a Revelation, or the Apocalypse, where there are the descriptions of the Seal of God and the Seal of Goddess.

Verse 9, of the first chapter of the book of A Revelation to John, John begins to give his testimony. "I, John, your brother and sharer with you in the tribulation and kingdom and endurance in company with Jesus, came to be in the isle that is called Patmos for speaking about God and bearing witness to Jesus." This verse implies Jesus was with John on the island of Patmos, at least in the spirit they were keeping each other company. And then, the vision begins.

John, the revelator is writing his farewell speech to the world, for he was going to be executed, or starved and used for hard labor until his death. He must have sensed that his final shining moment was at hand, and that now was time to reveal the vision he was given to the world. He must have been on the verge of breaking down and wanted to take a shot at the target, the hope he must have had in the kingdom of heaven, as a place that he, Jesus, and the rest were creating.

Jesus's and John's connection, our connection, your connection to God is supposed to work like God's own sworn oath to Abraham and promise to Noah. The Sovereign Seals given to Jesus by God is supposed to assist in the accomplishing of a nation of God's people, God's Children. What happened? How can the storm be calmed? The book of A Revelation is a letter from God, the Almighty, through time, coming through the words.

To reveal the Sovereign Seals, we will have to choose the book of a Revelation because it is the first and maybe the only book that is devoted to describing what the Seals look like. The combination of scripture with depictions, proofs and reproofs should propel the Sovereign Seals safe passage into some formal verbiage of spiritual law, Ecclesiastical law, much like the proscription constituted under the declaration of Divine Providence being proscribed to individual freedom, and governance with a path of protection of the divine rights of the Divine which proves to be in all things, because now the Real Seal provides us with a new view of who we are in the Kingdom of God, and what that means for other nations and individuals.

The claim of inalienable rights are on the right track. Perhaps, there will be a formal adoption of the Sovereign Seals by the people of the Earth. Hopefully, if there are survivors of the next "end times", the survivors can restart civilization with knowledge of the truth, and the Sovereign Seal will be the cornerstone of that new beginning of the Kingdom of Heaven.

Let us start looking into the first chapter of the book of A Revelation to John. Verse one says something astounding and very overlooked, very clearly, that Jesus is the author. "A Revelation by Jesus Christ", which God gave Jesus to show the people the things that will take place shortly. "And Jesus sent forth his angel and presented the revelation in signs through him to his slave John." Those first five words, "A Revelation by Jesus Christ," gives you the title, A Revelation, and the author, Jesus Christ. There is nowhere in scripture written that Jesus had slaves, perhaps John just felt about Jesus like Moses felt about JHVH, in his willingness to be of service.

Jesus's words are all throughout the New Testament, but A Revelation is the only book that practically, literally, has his name, titles, and seal, yet few if any Christians believe that Jesus wrote the book A Revelation. John is declared as the "witness", not the author. How did Jesus write the book, A Revelation, if he was dead, incapable of writing? Thus the reasoning behind the belief that John actually wrote the book, a Revelation.

Jesus had been prophesied about and then was born. He lived and preached the word, the way, also know as the Tao, then died, or, was put to death when he made his claim. After Jesus dies he was seen in a transfigured form that was not flesh and blood, but spirit. People could see, hear, and touch Jesus and his wounds were all gone.

Scripture implies after death Christ was assigned an Angel. In chapter one verse one of A Revelation, the same Angel is given the task of showing the Sovereign Seal to John in signs. Jesus then sends his Angel to bear witness, Revelation 22:16. There are many angels referenced in A Revelation and there is no way to know Christ's nameless angel from among one, two, seven, twelve, or the 144,000 mentioned.

Honestly, what can we use to unscramble our minds after reading the book of A Revelation, to John? A Revelation, chapter one, verse two - John "bore witness to the word God gave and to the witness Jesus Christ gave, yes, to all the things he saw." - is legal jargon for a big eventual, "I told you so.", possibility. Witnesses? Testimony of some kind, for a legal case.

A Revelation 1:3, "Happy is he who reads aloud and those who hear the words of this prophecy and who observe the things written in it; for the appointed time is near."

Verse three suggests, to read aloud this book, and be happy, because hearing the words of prophecy and observing the things written in the revelation is really important. The reason is because "the appointed time is near." Again, a judicial statement is made. Are you any happier when you read aloud? Can you remember what you have read out loud easier than when you read silently to yourself? Do you pray out loud or silently? If God answers your silent prayer, does that make Him a mind reader?

Chapter one, verse four of A Revelation, utilizes another judicial term describing "seven congregations in the 'district' of Asia." The number, seven is used for the first time in the book of a Revelation. In the first chapter the number seven is used ten times. The word seven appears fifty-eight times in A Revelation.

What was the district of Asia considered to be during the time when a Revelation was scribed? Who are the seven congregations? What purpose did they serve Jesus, John, and the early Christians? Are the seven congregations a discreet reference to the secret order of the Brotherhood of Seven that many of the ancient traditions secretively allude to in stories of the temple builders? Or, were the seven congregations seeds sown for a new nation founded by the apostles after their teacher died? Or, did Jesus personally set them up while alive? Did he already have that much of a following?

From the first few verses of A Revelation, we get the impression of some legal spiritually and lawfully contracted promise and a savior to deliver that promise to the people and the world. When Jesus died, God had to deal with His crisis. Killing Jesus was a prophecy, meaning something to be avoided, as when God's promise to Abraham occurred when God stopped Abraham from offering his son Isaac sacrificially, Genesis 21:1-4. Now, what is God to do with the people of the Earth? Sending Jesus was Plan A. Now, that he had passed, God quickly adjusted to Plans B, and C, the book of A Revelation and the Christian movement.

We could ask ourselves what a vision might be for God? Perhaps when Jesus was killed, God too passed out a little, for the sky was darkened at midday. Oh, the horror! Everything God had planned for Jesus for centuries was taken off of the table. Maybe the shock was too much, and God passed out briefly and had a vision. That vision He shared with Jesus, which became the Revelation. Scripture, history and myths are full of visions, visionaries, prophets, prophecies and prognosticators. Visions and voices are unique and there are categories and subcategories. The general theme of the plan, the promise of salvation marches on, even with Jesus dead, resurrected, and ascended, transfixing us in the balance.

Somewhere near Christ's place at the right hand of God, we can imagine an angel of God tells Jesus, "God, your Father had a vision, a revelation." Jesus received the vision and relayed the vision to his angel, who in turn relayed the vision to the Apostle John, who then scribed the vision for future generations. The book, A Revelation, is more than third hand news.

In verse five, chapter one of A Revelation, the introduction of the author continues, perhaps, in recognizable code words: "and from Jesus Christ, the Faithful Witness," "The first-born from the dead," and "Ruler of the kings of the earth." These are declarations of true testament from the dead and the living, from Jesus saying, "I rule over the rulers of the earth." Is A Revelation a deed of claim? Is the claim valid? Kings make claims to the title of king, and what that means is that they are claiming sovereignty.

A Revelation 1:5 is a list of titles, like a legal claim, declaring spiritual territorial titles. When Jesus said, "I and the Father are One.", in the Gospel of John, 10:30 makes more sense because the titles created for God and for Jesus, suddenly became infused, interchangeable.

Sovereignty is a claim, of a declarative nature, a legally functioning statement, an assertion. In Jesus's case, sovereignty means jurisdictional authority, which is what kings claim to have, the right to speak commands and be obeyed, to rule. Great freedom or great slavery results whenever one's own individual sovereignty is functioning. Freely we choose from the table what we eat, but as a slave we must excrete.

Continuing, verse five, "To him who loves us and has freed us from our sins by his blood, 6 and made us a kingdom, priests to his God and Father, to him be glory and dominion forever and ever. Amen."

Slaves are held in the chains of debt, the wealthy slaves to their wealth. Debt is presently gifted as liberty, freedom, and self-worth. Does God's Sovereignty present itself as giving each person a dollar value? Does His Sovereignty have anything to do with your value in currency, cold gold, hard paper cash, or digits on a plastic card? Does God meet you on the street or knock at your door and ask you to, "Tell me what you are worth?"

How much Hell can you take, like Job took, before you break? Is God testing us to find out what we're worth? Of course not, and yet, God's jurisdictional claim in the book of A Revelation, the Apocalypse of John, is only due to the "worthiness" of only three beings. The first is God, who is worthy because, Rev. 4:11, "You are worthy, JHVH, even our God, to receive the glory and the honor, and the power, because you created all things, and because of your will they existed and were created." Before the declaration by those around God's throne, they offer God glory, honor, and thanksgiving, and then, fall down before Him and caste their crowns before His throne. God is worthy because He created those around His throne, much like we revere our own parents. All the beings around the throne of God owe their very existence to His will, which is His power, and when His glory is realized by them, they, the created, realize their own glory, in the shared miracle of life and that moment in Heaven. God's glory is realized when we realize our glory is in having been created.

There is a list of promises and sworn oaths in scripture. One of the last promises is in A Revelation 10:6, when somebody swore, "there would be no delay." One of the sworn oaths that the scriptures, hands down, is all about, is that someday, somebody, would prove God's Sovereignty in Heaven was being extended and offered to the people, all people on Earth, equally. From then on, all human claims have no relevance and cannot be enforced, unless derived from their common source, their common equity in their common sovereignty, as Children of the Most High God and Most High Goddess.

The second one who is worthy of praise is described in A Revelation 5:6, and looks like, "a lamb as though it had been slaughtered, having seven horns and seven eyes, which mean the seven spirits,". Is the lamb a composition of someone created by God or a description of what we might find hidden in the Sovereign Seal? Could the lamb be one of the seven spirits before the throne of God?

There is already a lion there at the throne, but cats get nine lives to realize their purr-fection. We may have but one life to realize our sovereignty by realizing God's Sovereignty. How are we to find a seven-eyed, seven-horned, semi-rendered lamb in this meat market of a world, when we can barely find our way home?

The third worthy person is the bride, the Queen, Our Common Mother, A Revelation 12:1, who has "a crown of twelve stars", which is the Goddess's Sovereign Seal. Our notion of self-worth is at issue and we get these notions from our surroundings and our interactions, but the Sovereign Seal was unbeknownst to us and can change everything, as we realize the glory, we become that glory. When we realize God's Sovereignty, we become sovereign, glorified, honored, and become ourselves, without castigation.

From the cradle to the grave we suffer, we are tested, and we are judged. According to the scriptures the tests began right away to inquire as to our value and the virtue of our existence. As in Job, or as in the temptations of Jesus Christ, among many stories, even the story of the Buddha, we are all being put to a test of trials, tribulations and sufferings, all because of the actions of the most wicked and evil of all of the "fallen angels", whose motive we know not, but to speculate the fallen angels seek to deny us our glory, God's sovereignty, and God's glory. What happens if we fail in the commission God gave us, to have dominion, sovereignty over ourselves, which the fallen angels have been denying God?

Perhaps, that "angel" or Devil, Satan, did such a good job of wiping out and erasing men like Job, Jesus, and John the Baptist, that the issue of God's dominion went unnoticed, and God's Sovereignty was almost left completely out of the Scriptures, poetry, ideology, and politics. For, if God is Sovereign, who needs a king, a pharaoh, a judge, a lawyer, a governor, or a priest? Our lives mean something, or they mean nothing. Realizing God's Sovereignty in our lives, with God's Seal, as proof of our sovereignty, we become an extension of God's Sovereignty, and again may become free to discover for ourselves what sovereignty means. We can all claim equality amongst ourselves in God's Sovereignty and then sit down on our own little thrones.

God has dominion over Heaven and Earth. We need to realize God's Sovereignty in all of our actions in order to be in His Sovereignty, in harmony with God while we live on Earth in Heaven, and share in His Sovereignty which gives us sovereignty. If we deny the Most High there is the possibility that the cock would crow three more times, and the little red hen would have to do all the work until Saint Peter decides he would like to cook the hen for his Last Supper and have some of the bread she made. In Matthew, Chapter 26, verse 34, 74 and 75, what Peter denied was Jesus and the Sovereign, sent by God to establish the Kingdom of God's Sovereignty, here on Earth. And raven or rooster, some cock crowed, as if in victory like a devil, something Jesus forewarned Peter of. If Jesus already had the Sovereign Seal while alive, certainly he would have shown it to Peter and the rest of the Apostles. Perhaps, if Peter had seen the Sovereign Seal he would have openly confessed to knowing Jesus.

The Aquarian Gospel of Jesus Christ, by Eliphas Levi, implies that Joseph, Jesus's "father", was a rabbi of the religious sect known as the Essenes, who were one of seven secret brotherhoods of the Sacred Secret Brotherhood of Seven, which had put together seven secret schools for the initiation of seven tests of worthiness to find the Son of God. Jesus was the first to pass all seven initiation tests, from all seven schools, and was supplied the innermost teachings of the Sacred Secret Brotherhood of Seven. After passing all of the tests Jesus was given the recognized right to be claimed and to claim himself: "King of Israel", "King of the Jews", "Messiah", "Savior", "Son of God", and other titles, some of which have been posthumously imparted to him. Then, Jesus was baptized and the Devil came to test him.

With Jesus gone the devil danced and celebrated his continuing torment of those on Earth, under Heaven. The history of horror continued for a thousand years, plus, almost a thousand more. Then, the devil found us nuking, blowing up the world he wanted for himself.

The feeling of a new world beginning encourages me to experience the freedom to print, and give praise for God, but hold myself responsible as specially chosen by my grandfather to assist the liberation of the Seal to those in America, first, which seemed predestined by the compulsion of the idea of spiritual equity, in God's Sovereignty, in God's eyes, for each individual, which is declared in the founding documents of America. The

American Constitution allows a person to be free, without bowing down to any god, angel, demon, devil, judge, king, queen, emperor, priest-king, banker, or any other slave-maker who dares to claim ownership and sovereignty over others. An American is different. An American is supposed to stand, at the ready, as long as they can, then, eventually, fall down and die and is never, ever to bow down to receive equality, which is given as a right, by God, in the Constitution, that we live by the truth of freedom given by God, the Creator, and our mothers and fathers, proclaiming sovereignty for ourselves, for God, and for future generations.

I have picked nits and scratched my head like a monkey, but this fellow Jesus, has John go on, to bless Jesus with further introductory, "To him that loves us and that loosed us from our sins by means of his own blood… 6 and he made us to be a kingdom of priests to his God and Father… yes, to him be the glory and the might forever. Amen." Revelation 1:7 states, "Look! He is coming with the clouds, and every eye will see him, and those who pierced him; and all the tribes of the earth, will beat themselves in grief because of him. Yes, Amen."

Remember, Adam the first man, was created perfect and given some sovereignty over certain realities of the world. In essence he was the first father, king, chief, wise man, first elder and oldest elder. According to scripture, Adam was made to "have in subjection the fish of the sea and the flying creatures of the heavens and the domestic animals and all the earth and every moving animal that is moving upon the earth." Genesis: 1:26. Then God said, in Gen.: 1:29, "Here I have given to you all vegetation bearing seed which is on the surface of the whole earth and every tree on which there is the fruit of a tree bearing seed. To you let it serve as food. And to every wild beast of the earth and to every flying creature of the heavens and to everything moving upon the earth in which there is life as a soul I have given all green vegetation for food. And it came to be so." Adam was given sovereignty over a great amount of stuff.

Adam made a mistake, or for some reason was considered an imperfect, fallen, exiled being. Jesus symbolized the re-perfection of man, man reborn as God. However, was the reinstitution of the Sovereign Seal supposed to be a part of a new nation, a new kingdom of Heaven on Earth? Was Jesus's political ideology a throwback to an original view of what was once called the 'paradise' of God?

The fact is my ancestors and your ancestors have been around a long time and we all have a common ancestor, God, so anyone else's right of claim and jurisdictional sovereignty over anything but themselves, if they are free, is a bold face lie.

The idea of God's Sovereignty is revealed in Genesis, throughout the scriptures and in a Revelation to John, the Apocalypse. In the book of Genesis, God's Sovereignty is described in the First seven days and seven nights of creation, and in the promise of God to Abraham, 22:16-18. From Buddha to the Tao te Ching, in Islam and in the geometries of old, many emblems, symbols, or seals, like the star of David and the Seal of Solomon can be found in the Sovereign Seal. The Sovereign Seal of God and Goddess have been completely missing from the Earth, until now.

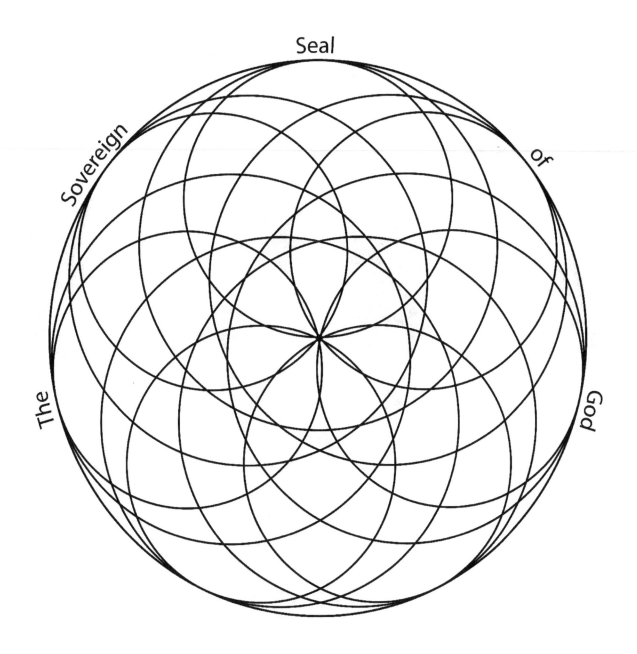

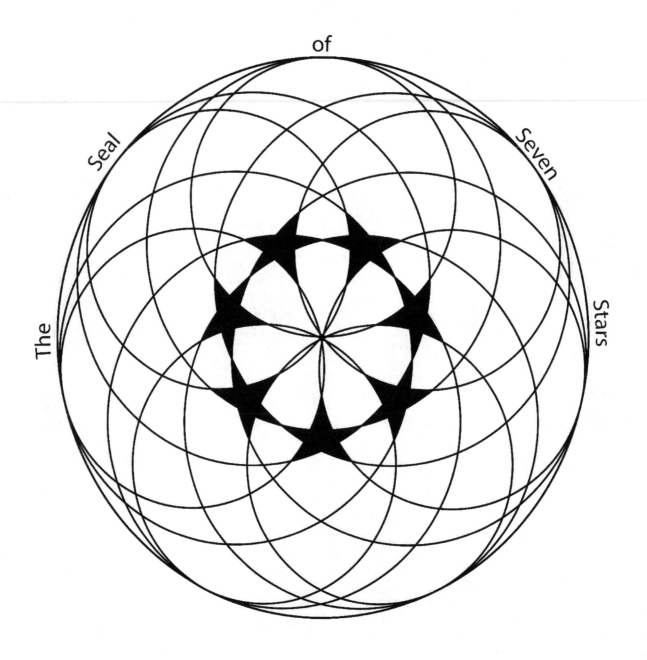

The Seal of Seven Stars

A Revelation 2:1, "These are the things he says who holds the seven stars in his right hand."

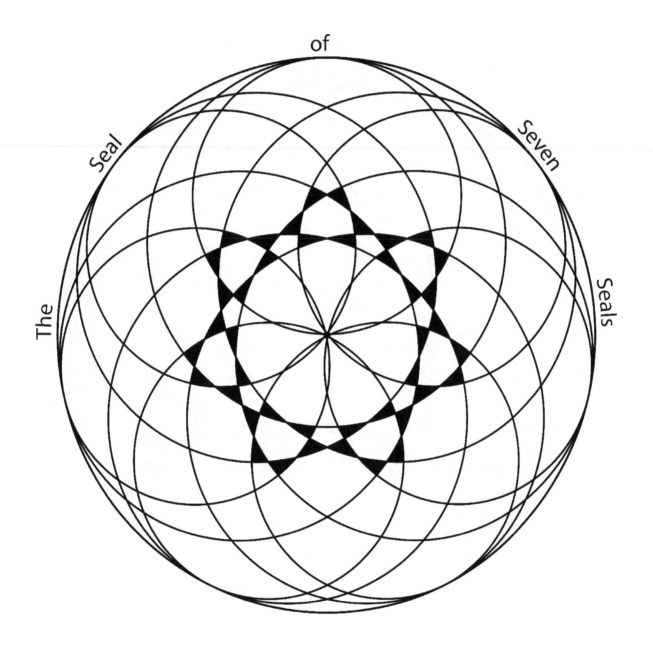

The Star of David, currently emblazoned on the flag of Israel, appears in the Sovereign Seals. You can find descriptions of the Sovereign Seal in A Revelation Chapters five and six.

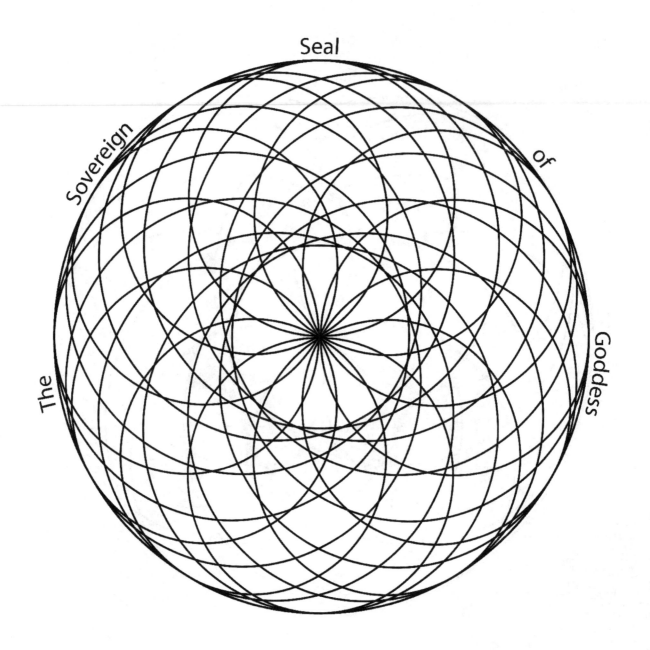

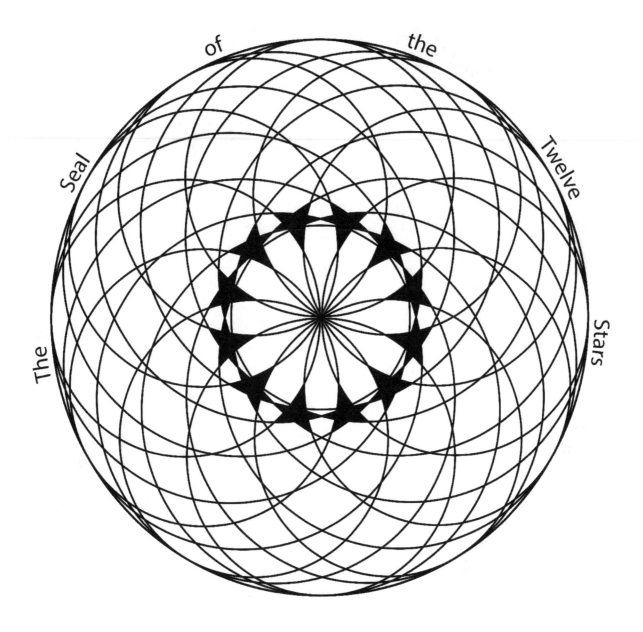

The Seal of the Twelve Stars

A Revelation 12:1, "A woman was arrayed with the sun, and the moon was beneath her feet, and on her head was a crown of twelve stars."

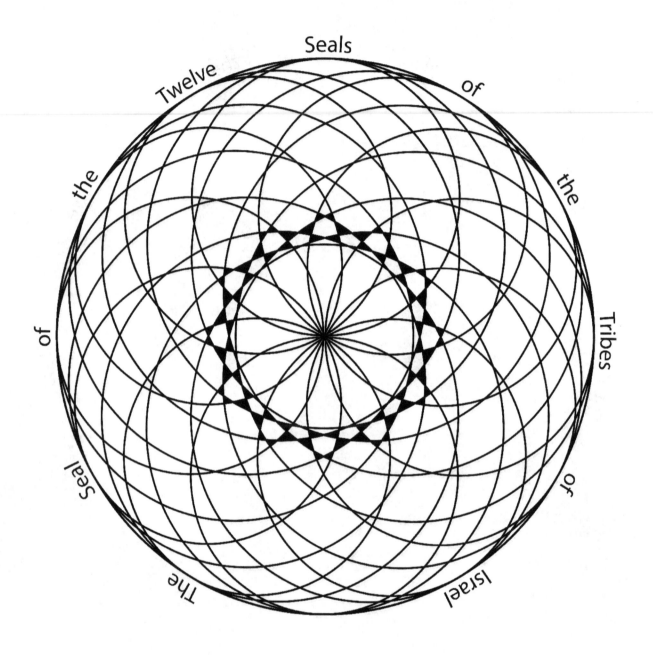

The number twelve seems to be the main theme in the description of the New Jerusalem found in A Revelation Chapter 21 verses 10 through 21.

"For no matter how many the promises of God are, they have become yes by means of him. Therefore, also through him is the Amen said to God for glory through us. 21 But he who guarantees that you and we belong to Christ and he who has anointed us is God. 22 He has also put his seal upon us and has given us the token of what is to come, that is, the spirit, in our hearts.", Second Corinthians 1:20.

All of the slave-like followings of the grand religions started with a person, a prophet, given a seal for their followers to identify each other with and to provide some structure and identity for that people. These seals came from a common heavenly source, not of an evil or alien source, but an 'angel', usually in the sky, and is Our Common Mother. When men would meet Our Common Father for inspiration and leading the people, Heaven turns around and the sun sits at its high point. The men trembling are too terrified and usually ashamed of themselves, because God brings Heaven's whole army with Him when He appears, and the thunder and lightning which makes the individual more inclined to fear God for His Almighty stature, then love Him for being a great Father to the billions of spirits who cling to Him and His throne for life.

The sacred symbols of the prophets, for some reason, were deemed worthy to receive an aspect of the Sovereign Seal, an aspect of sovereignty from on High. Some of the prophets we know by the names of Mohammed, Jesus, the Buddha, Lao Tzu, Abraham, Zoroaster, and others. Their emblems, seals, sigils or symbols are for territorial jurisdictional sovereignty which still exist today in many of the same regions. These symbols are everywhere on flags, and currency and are used to make documents officially living laws that if disobeyed result in penalties such fines, incarceration, or death.

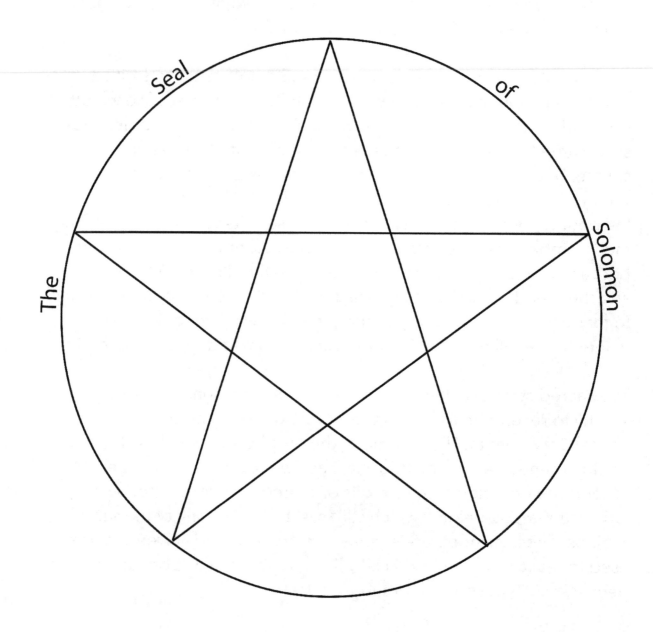

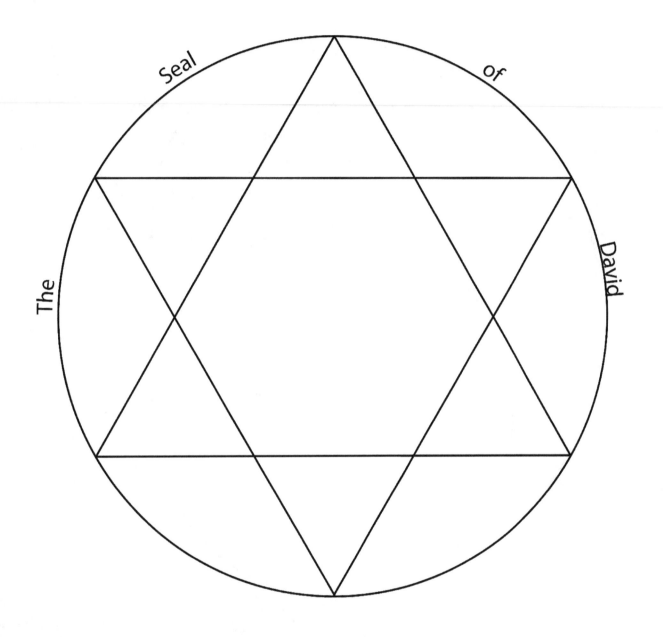

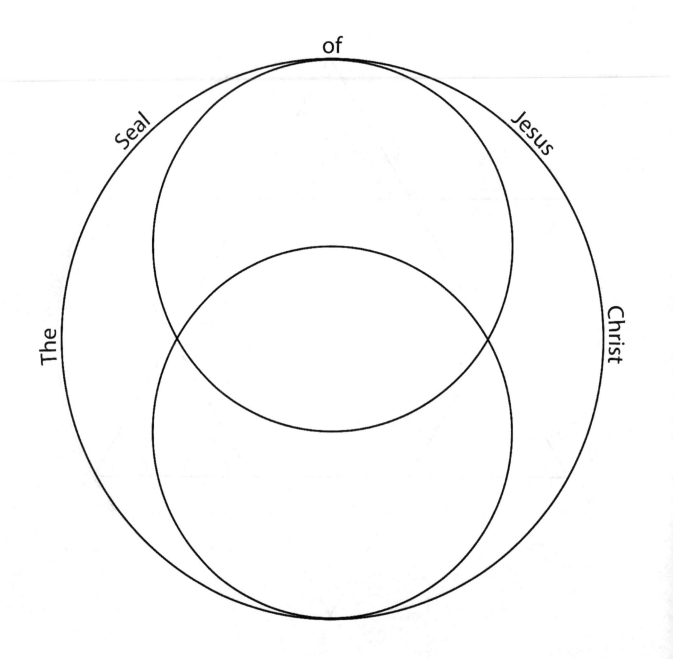

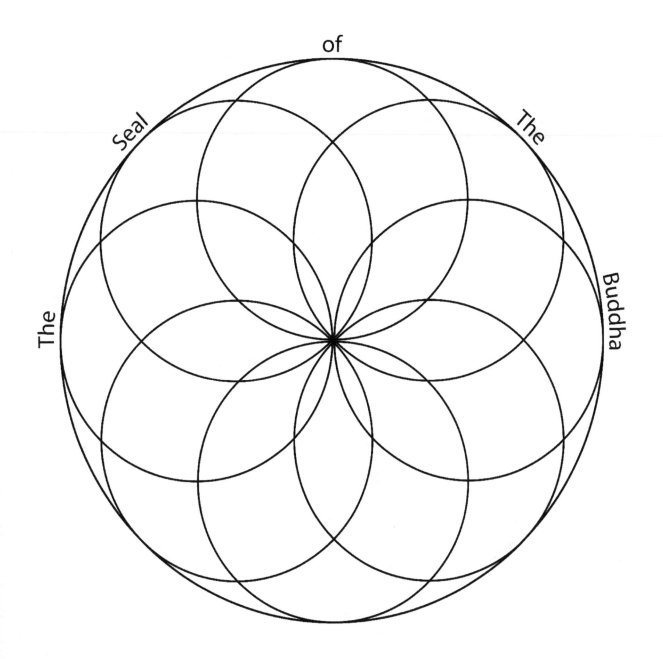

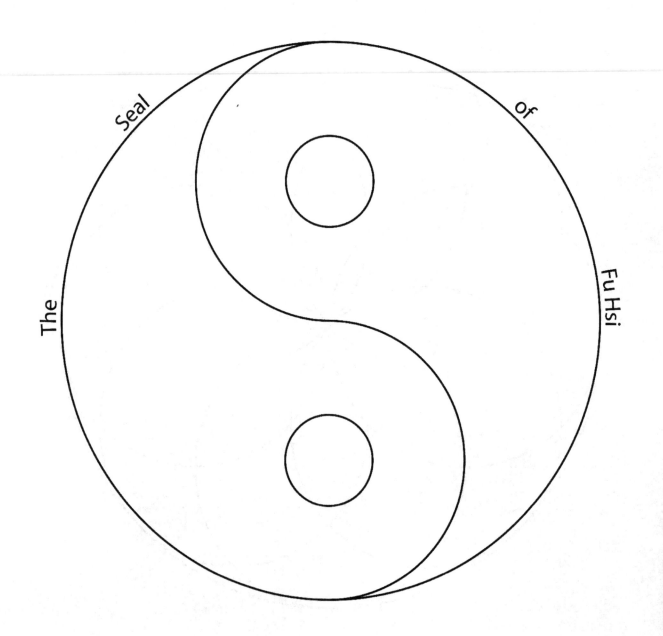

The Seal of Fu Hsi

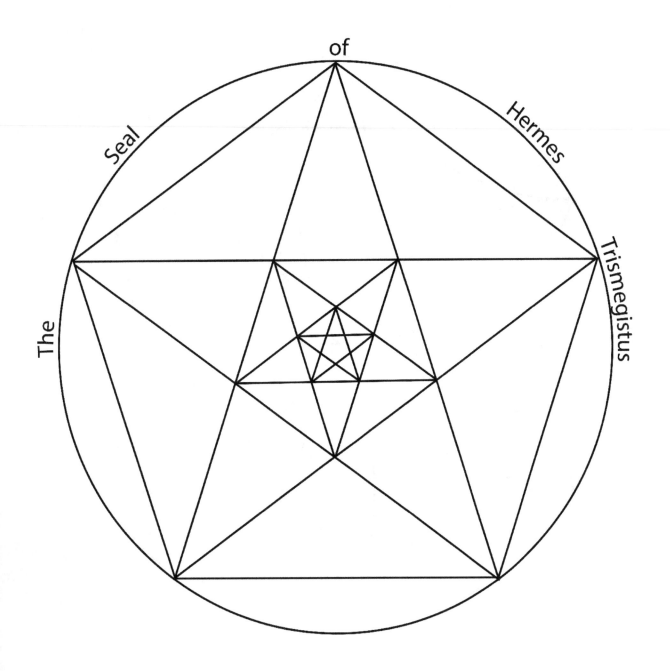

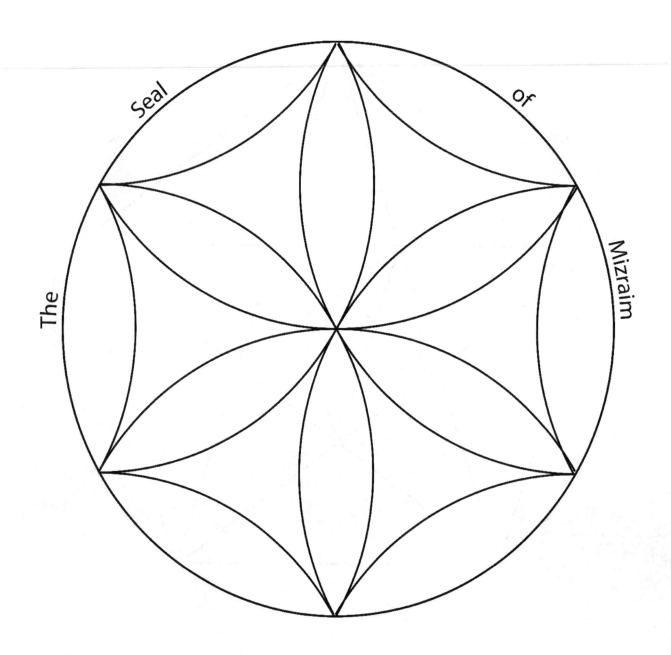

The Seal of Mizraim

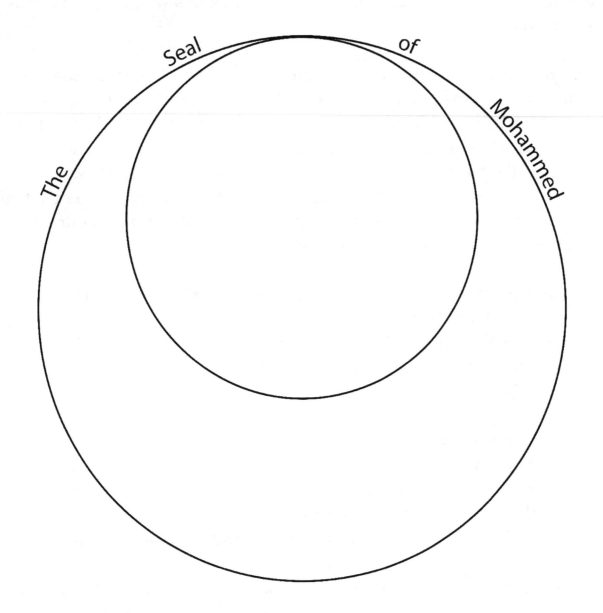

88

Sometimes the holy symbols are put directly into the architecture and the artwork of a people whose culture is or was at one time influenced by one of the prophets of God. The arched entrances of most Christian churches and cathedrals are half of the Vesica Pisces. In the paintings of sacred individuals, they are often painted inside of a whole Vesica Pisces called a mandorla.

The symbols given to the prophets are pieces of the Sovereign Seal and must come together, fit together, work together, which would be the essence of the meaning of the Sovereign Seal for us all: "Work together." God is speaking directly to us. If you put the symbols together the Holy symbol of the Most High is revealed, which means if we do not work together, we are doomed. Each seal given to the prophets is a part in the creation and function of God's promise of the scriptures about our salvation, here, now, and in the future.

Each time a prophet like Jonah is given a commission it is a test for the prophet. The sacred individuals who get pushed by compulsion from the Most High to the struggle for perfection, correction, salvation and enlightenment, are given a seal or symbol, for their identity becomes sacred to God.

You can see the seals or symbols of the prophets in the Sovereign Seals, proving that God has been working on revealing the Sovereign Seals for a very long time. Every one of the sacred individuals, the prophets, implied that there were those possessed by a source of great evil. The Sovereign Seal revelation means that that paradigm of evil rule ended.

Mohammed was given a crescent moon and sun Seal which sometimes is accompanied with a five-pointed star shining along with the sun and moon. The Sun of Day, Moon of Night and a bright star are brought together like something seen in a vision so powerful and beautiful that Mohammed deemed his vision relevant enough to use for his commission, as if given from Above, from God or an angel. Was the crescent moon and sun seal given to Mohammed as a covenant between

God and Mohammed, like when 'The Great' Constantine had a dream or a vision of the Flaming Cross that he had painted on shields before the battle for Susa?

Maybe one day Mohammed saw the crescent moon hug the sun and a star was born or maybe there was a triple alignment of sun, moon, and Venus that he saw that compelled him to feel an extraordinary vibration of peace. There are emblems like the grand conjunction carved on stone all over the world. The flower of life mandala and the swastika was carved on stone all over the world long before Jesus ever walked on water, or his people used the secret sign of a fish to identify each other.

Certain emblems or seals fit into the Sovereign Seal of the Most High. The Seal of Islam, the Seal of the fish, the Vesica Pisces of the early Christians, the six-pointed Seal of David currently on the flag of Israel, the lotus flower of the Buddha, and the Yin Yang symbol Seal of Fu Hsi which is currently on the flag of South Korea are all visible in the Sovereign Seal of the Most High, as if God and Goddess have been giving out pieces of the Sovereign Seals over time and throughout history, hoping that someday the mystery of the scroll of the seven seals would be solved and the people of the world become conscious of themselves as God's Children. Usually a prophet's seal comes along with a great teaching, inspirational words, songs and celebrations.

Before and after the crucifixion of Jesus, his apostles had a secret symbol in the form of a 'fish', the 'eye' of God. Inside the 'eye', 'all-seeing', is where the universe grows and is created and sustained by love, contained by cosmic law between the centers of the cosmic duality, in a unity. Christ's symbol is in the Sovereign Seals. The yin yang symbol given by either Fu Hsi or Lao Tzu is also in the Sovereign Seals, as well as the crescent moon and sun monopole Seal given Mohammed and also, the lotus bloom Seal given to the Buddha is in the Sovereign Seal.

Israel flies a hexagon star, a six-pointed star in a blended duality of two equilateral triangles. King David who may have borrowed the six-pointed star from the even older seal, called the flower of life. The six-point seal is thought by many to have been passed on to Solomon, David's adopted son.

Some sources say the five-pointed star with a circle around the star is the Seal of Solomon, and some say the Seal of Solomon is the Star of David, the six-pointed star. Israel's national flag, bearing the six-pointed star, flies as a symbol of the promise of God to all nations to bless themselves, Genesis 22:18. The six-pointed star is made of two interlocking equilateral triangles, and is called a hexad or hexagram which forms a hexagon inside of the six equilateral triangles, which can be folded inside the hexagon. Similarly, a pentagon is inside every pentacle, ad infinitum.

Some sources are in conflict, as to, whether or not, the Seal of Solomon had a five or six-pointed star. The Seal of Solomon is a decorative Jewish symbol, having a five-pointed star whose every point touches a circle and is also called the "Seal of Jacob", compared to the six-pointed "Star of David" which is a modern Jewish symbol.

The diagram of the Seal of Islam is the smiling sun and the broad smile is the crescent moon, a circle within a circle, seven of which converge at the center making the Sovereign Seal, as Goddess revealed to me, the seer, revealing Her connection to the origin of Islam, offering a color scheme of what is white like the moon and yellow like the sun, for both the sun and moon are at her feet in A Revelation. 12:1. Jesus spoke in the Gospels and in the book of A Revelation, the Apocalypse of John, of the Sovereign Seals of God, Maker of the expanse "Heaven", and of Goddess, the dry land "Earth".

When the prophets saw God, or someone sent by God or Goddess, a seal was given marking the event that something really big changed to such a degree as to engender in the prophets a compulsion or will of greater spirit. They see God and realize God as the Maker of all things including the prophet, and so must endure life as one who cannot separate their mind, heart, spirit, soul, and their whole being from being changed, influenced by God the Being. The prophets must apply some golden cause to effect rule to the greater reality, the world-at-large, when living in the service of God.

Fairy tales often talk of love, quests to prove worthiness, and the favorite tales always end, supposedly, "and they lived happily ever after."

What "happily ever after" means is never defined. Therefore, no one knows what "happily ever after" is or means. What would happily ever after mean for Jesus and the Christians, Buddha and the Buddhists, Mohammed and the Moslems? Are they not each very different, having very different views of what happily ever after means? And doesn't 'ever after' mean forever? Eternally speaking; happiness is without sadness, death, tragedy or violence.

There are others who have seals or symbols given them, the Sacred Hoop of many native indigenous American peoples, the Tibetan Wheel of Time, Seal of Atlantis and many others come to mind. However, only some of them can be derived or used to derive the Sovereign Seal of God or the Goddess Seal. The many seals we have been speaking about all seem to be from a common teaching of sacred geometry, the real language of the universe.

A Revelation 7:1, "After this I saw four angels standing upon the four corners of the earth, holding tight the four winds of the earth,". Zechariah 2:6, "For in the direction of the four winds of the heavens I have spread you people abroad," is the utterance of JHVH." Later in Chap. 6:1-7, talks about a vision of four chariots, four kinds of horses, and the four spirits of the heavens and which of the four directions they go.

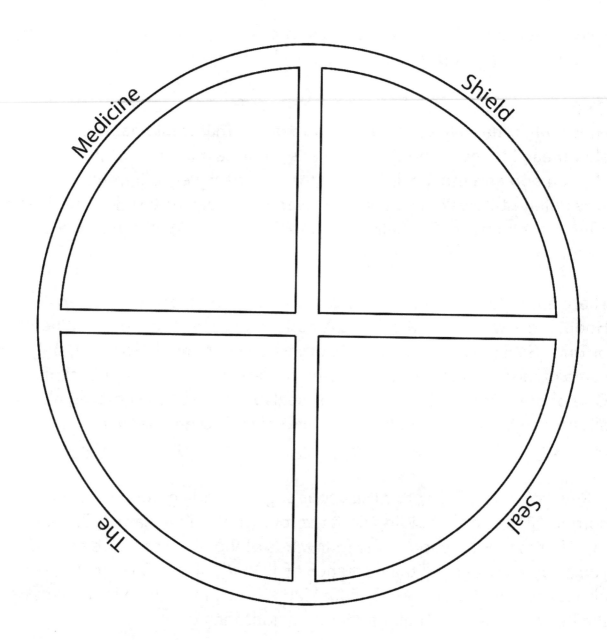

Adad was like Poseidon, the Sumerian God of storms who carried a trident. The Atlanteans might be where we get the protracted compass of 360 degrees to a circle. The concentric rings of the Seal of Atlantis are like the annual rings found when a tree is cut. Everything seems to be made of circles or rings, from wedding rings to the rings of Jupiter's pole, the rings of Saturn's equator and the hexagonal rings of its pole. One of the uses of the Seal of Atlantis is to wake up the third eye, also called the mind's eye, expressing the spiritual traveling through time and space, worm-holing, dreaming, passage through the center of the image.

The Seal of Atlantis, of Poseidon, an alien god-king, according to Plato, implies a shared knowledge of ancient peoples with alien peoples from the stars, and the polemics of possible 'human' origins from humans having sex with some other-worldly peoples, star peoples, producing the hybrids that God wanted wiped out by the flood. When you add the crossbars, from the sacred hoop to the Seal of Atlantis two images take form, the indigenous shaman drum, and a directional 'guidance' system for traveling the land, the seas, skies, and maybe 'space', the starry heavens.

Guidance for freedom of control and movement needs the center of gravity to stay centered from different vantage points, perspectively, something balanced can appear imbalanced. Whereas a top view of a monopole produces, the Seal of Atlantis, a general image of an island either rising from or sinking into the ocean, from a different perspective the monopole appears more like the seal of Islam. The seal of Islam looks like the center of gravity, the smallest circle, is touching the outer ring, and looks lopsided somewhat. The center of gravity appears like an object rounding a curve while tunneling or traveling.

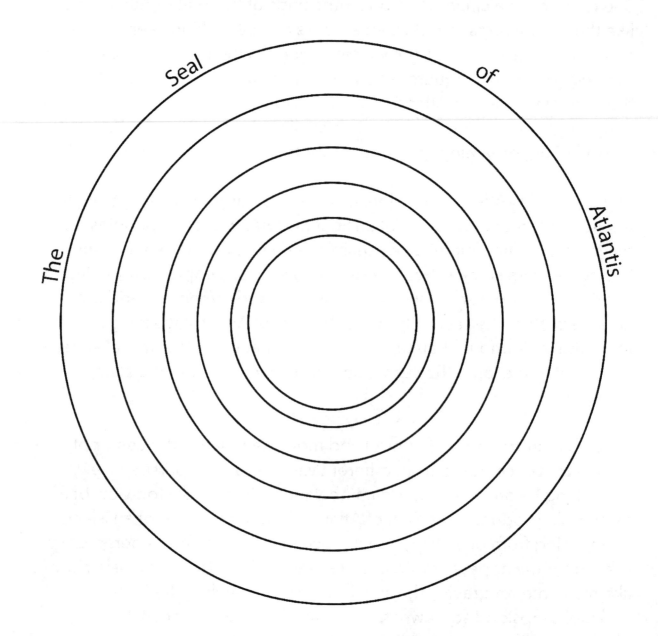

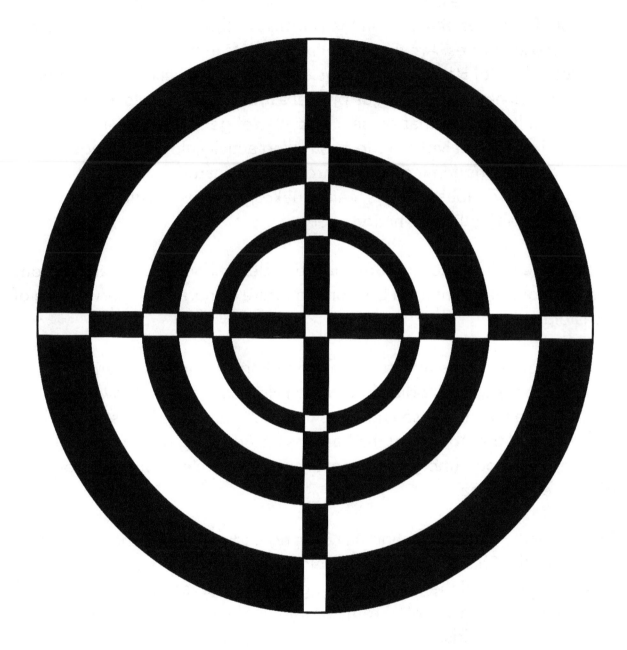

When the Medicine Shield is added to The Seal of Atlantis, the image looks more like a multi-directional guidance system for a spaceship.

The recurrence of a destructive cycle in the journey of the Earth through the Astrophysical Ages of the Heavens seems to be known to some of the most ancient cultures, those who intentionally made astrology the highest of sciences. Stars are in the promise at the beginning and at the end of the scriptures. Are there two fixed points in the stars of the elliptical wheel of Heaven that draws the ellipse, as Euclid did? The two points would have been seen as pivotal astrophysical points in the drawing of the ellipse that causes the cycles of geo-physically intense upheaval and apocalyptic world destroying activity, floods, ice ages, volcanic eruptions, famines, strikes from stellar material, typhoons, hurricanes, tornadoes, twisters, earthquakes, plagues, pestilence, pandemics, and other extinction events.

Knowledge of the recurring destructive cycles of Earth were derived from the survivors who sent forth beacons to future generations forewarning of disaster.

Ancient peoples were able to impart their knowledge in the form of sacred geometry, the Zodiac from which Horoscopes are derived, and the mandala teaching also known as the circle teaching. The story in the Precession of the Ages, is of the Earth as an Ark, a big boat, sailing like the crescent moon upon the ocean, around the circle of the starry oceans of the Celestial Sea.

The old ones, called the mandala teaching and still call it, "the medicine shield", or the Shield Teaching, in which the different tribes were given different aspects of the whole teaching which when brought together formed the "sacred secret". From combining the oldest family templates, their crests or shields, and their sigils or seals, these implements served for the remembrance of the ancestors, and the stories they told allowed for the teaching of the star shields to be passed on to future generations by their elders. "We are star people." The elders have the stories to tell and also their own stories to remember. I think that remembering for the people, and remembering one's own life, is wisdom. The wisdom and the practice of self-remembering may slow down the aging process. Giving one's being relevance consciously is important to crystalize one's spirit and edify one's soul.

According to ancient oral traditions we come from the stars. Are we literally star people?

The Mayan stories tell a tale of a "Lord Shield" defending the people from a "Lord Bat". Some of the ancient stories were so important that they were written and became the Holy Scriptures. The medicine shield or mandala teaching can be found in the Holy Scriptures, supposedly direct from oral tradition. Genesis 15:1, ". . . I am a shield to you.", the words tie themselves to the oral traditions associated to survivors of the flood, the fire, and the freeze, in the time of the Age of Leo when our ancient ancestors chanced upon the realization that the cause of the destructive effects on Earth were previously written in the stars.

Our ancestors, who lived long lives, set to the godly task of the monolithic temple building which warns of an even older time in the precession, during Aquarius when the preceding ancestors spoke of the same tumult of sufferings, and discovered a cycle, a cycle of destruction, written in the stars occurring at opposite ends of the ellipse of the Zodiac. Information pertaining to the ordeals of the people who were resolved to endure in God's covenant, to be "a shield", something that protects is almost voided out of scripture. The shields were skins dried like a drum on a hoop and painted with a sigil. They were not, drums. They were not used in battle.

Many cultures, like that of the Akkadians, the Hittites, the Babylonians, Chaldeans, and Sumerians, were using seals of various kinds for a few thousand years, as the written word slowly began to develop.

The scriptures and the use of seals come from the same region of the world where written language developed. Indo-European letters and alphabets like Greek, Hebrew and Phoenician, originated from Sanskrit and spread west and north by Aryans moving out from the Indus River Valley region around 1200 B.C. The Indic language was used for writing the religious and literary works of India.

In Hinduism, the Yantra is a graphic visualization of divine force of the Goddess Shri manifest as Shakti, and is the symbolic visualization of unity with Brahma unfolding as multiplicity. The Yantra image is used to meditate on for it reveals meaning and speaks to the mind and soul. Such art is called holy, because of how the art impacts an organic sense of something divine. The Tibetan "Wheel of Time" mandala is one of the most miraculous and very best geometric expressions which creates the magic illusion of three-dimensional projections from a two-dimensional surface called the Mandala Effect.

"The Yantra"

"The Tibetan Wheel of Time"

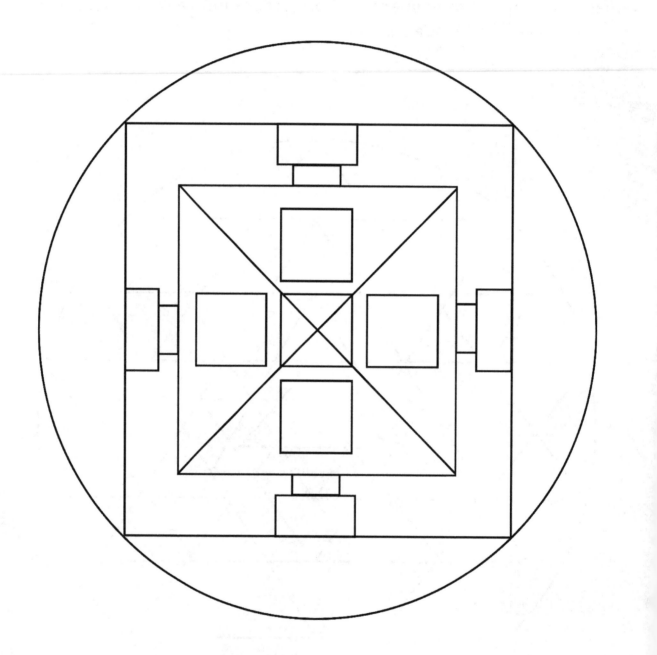

On the next few pages are examples of how really good mandala drawings produce magical or miraculous impressions, where what is a 2-dimensional drawing produces 3- dimensional images. Are these hallucinations? No, because others can see them and validate what is being seen.

The ancestral and spiritual virtue of the common universal revelation in the mandala teaching unites all beings above and below, for the mandala teaching is a common universal revelation, a teaching available to all beings of 'higher' being consciousness which liberates them all to maintain a sense of the One within All, and liberates the One to maintain a sense of Itself within All, thus uniting the One with the All, one and all, in the Glory of the One.

One of the most ancient disciplines teaches the common cosmic comprehension of life through the application of the great mandala teaching. In the ancient art of mandala making, the mandalas depict the ordinal structure of everything. Knowing the universal laws depicted by mandalas are essential in understanding creation, all things, lifting the veil of creation in all living things, and our spiritual and scientific ignorance. The mandala teaching, also called the Holy of Holies in which the Sovereign Seal revelation is found speaks to us as a real spiritually integrated universal common cosmic truth.

The Holy of Holies is the original teaching given 'man' kind, through the use of circles, where the dala, in mandala, means great, for man is great in the eyes of God. In The Holy of Holies, The Mandala Teaching, each circle represents a law, a being, a number, creating and maintaining creation on all scales of being. Thus we say each mandala is a law and is where we get the idea of God's Law being circular, all-encompassing, all-loving, all-knowing, and all the rest. In The Mandala Teaching, God is a circle. Goddess is a circle. Each circle is a mandala and each mandala, is a law, an ordinal god.

"Om mani padme hom"
The Jewel is in the Lotus

Central to the Buddhists is the Jewel, the Holy Lotus Seal, the Seal of Buddha, which is a mandala. The universal law of nature expressed in the Seal of Buddha is the law of unblended duality.

Lotus Floating on the Water

The lotus from a side view further explores how the laws of the universe, nature's laws, manifest in reality.

If you find that you absolutely must believe in something, all belief and knowledge is reduced to the possibility of the One being miraculous and that miracle spoken of as the word or the Prime Move, the first cause uncaused, is still happening and we are just a part of a miracle, living in the Infinite Miraculous because of the miraculous-ness of the One, the Most High as the ancients call the First Being, Free, for it came from nothing and so do we. All things move toward singularities of principles while moving from previous singularities, like Time, probability, the limits of God's will.

Our mandala study is what systematically led us to the discovery of the Sovereign Seals. The word "mandala" is Sanskrit for circle. Mandalas, circles, from their inception have been used for the creation of seals. The use of a Seal is for jurisdictional sovereignty, a deed of claim through declarative law to take possession of land, people, their possessions, and to enforce under penalty of death or imprisonment any sealed commands or laws. "Enclosing the face of the throne, Spreading out over it his cloud. He has described a circle upon the face of the waters, To where light ends in darkness." Job 26:9. Mandala art is a living breathing artform where by drawing the outer most circle, activates a seal legally, and breathes the breath of life into the image inside. The image rises from the two-dimensional plane into the third dimension.

Scriptures were originally oral traditions, memorized, usually sung, in rounds, called "mandalas", for the telling of the stories of the people. Huge stone glyphs depicted sculpted images of the chiefs, orators, shamans, elders and bards used to remember and tell the "gospels" of their people to successive generations. Scripture put those words and images from those stories recollected into the documents that the people call, as they have from of old, "the Word of God".

The common mandala of love, or the blended duality was used for the construction of Noah's Ark, as per God's instruction, Genesis 6:14. Proportions for the length and width of the Ark fit exactly inside the classic image of the fish, Christ's Seal, the 'eye' of God.

Noah's Ark is an exact design so that any wave would roll over the craft without rolling the craft over. The symbol of blended duality became a secret sign for Christians being persecuted in early Christian times called the fish, Vesica Pisces, the ichthymus, or Jonah's whale. Without suspicion, early Christians would slyly draw an arc in the dirt with their foot. If another person walked over nonchalantly and drew the other arc, the first person knew the other was Christian. Just as the law of unblended duality, Buddha's Seal, The Jewel, is a universal law expressed in all things, the universal law of blended duality, Jesus's Seal, the Fish also known as the Eye, is also expressed, and being expressed by all things, even the Sovereign Seals of Goddess and God.

The blended and unblended dualities are the two fundamental cosmic laws absolutely expressed in all things. Not only do they form the Seals, and are forming all things, and giving them life, they get us closer to understanding how a universe may be something we might be able to create on our own scale of existence, and literally give one as a gift to someone. Would receiving a gift like a universe fill your sense of being divine, maybe like a god or goddess?

Apocalyptic literature is prophecy. Prophesy is foresight. If everything comes to an end, all worlds, things, even universes, how might we know the end? By creating a universe on our own scale of existence we can observe the end. Will the universe we live in end the same way. If so, we might know and have the foresight to prophesy the exact moment to say, "Farewell? Goodbye?" Nothing quite seems apropos.

First, we need to figure out what kind of a warped matrix the Earth is. We must not let our minds play tricks on us. The mandala teaching reveals a warping impression, which makes something two-dimensional, like the Jewel, Seal of Buddha, begin to breathe and a three-dimensional appearance of a lotus flower occurs in our mind even though the drawing is flat and round. Earth seems like a globe, but also seems to be flat, just like the Mandala Effect. Is Earth a warping mandala which allows us to see the Earth in both a two-dimensional and a three-dimensional image?

She mothered universes. He studied them, watching, and listening to them with his heart.

In his mind he thought, "I can make one and hold it in my hands."

He studied the stars, the infinitely large, the macroscopic and the microscopic, the infinitely small, things on all scales of being.

Then He created some in his lab in the basement. The universes He made He gave to Her.

She held one in each hand and the universes each took a breath. They began to sparkle then flew away and disappeared.

He looked at her, shocked. "They are alive!", he shouted, the look of realization on his face.

"What did you think?", she asked.

His mind was blown. He was in awe. "Well, then, what am I?" He asked insisting. "You must be the one who created me!?"

"But, I thought that you made me.", She said.

They looked quizzingly into each other's faces and moved in a circle around each other, first clockwise, then, counter-clockwise, and a portal opened connecting their minds, and It too, flew away.

From Thoth to Hermes, to Pythagoras, to Solomon, all of the way to the Templars, the image of a star inside a star, inside another star, is seen as an expression of the law of infinitude, where in the macrocosmic we find the same laws as in the microcosmic, and is proof for the thesis found in the Emerald Tablets of Thoth or Hermes Trismegistus.

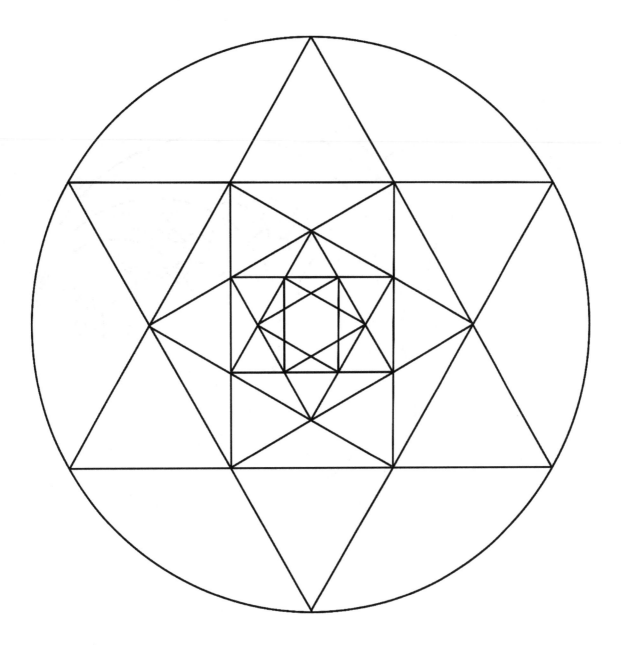

A geometrical expression of the universal law of infinitude.

"And now the saints go marching in with the Sovereign Seals. Hoo-Ra!"

You pleaded for freedom though I did not cage you. I opened the cage and set you free. After a while you came out but then went back in and closed the cage.

I found you chained, locked away, and set you free. You put the chains on and threw away the key.

I found you lost at sea, sure to drown, and rescued you. You jumped back in the sea.

I put you back into the Garden of Paradise and you ran back to Hell.

I shouted at you, "you do not have to die to live in Heaven!"

And you called for the ship, the key, freedom from the cage, and returned to Heaven even though you live on Earth. You called for your father and mother. You called for your family. You called for God. He sent his son. You sent him back and asked God for another. God calls you back and says:

"I call upon you."

You answer, "Oh hell no! I'm free."

I showed you the Sovereign Seal of the Most High. I offered all that I promised, and you refused my gift. But hell is no more child, and though I rest my feet on Earth, it is in Heaven. The Seals prove this is so. You rest your feet on Earth which cannot be taken away from you. When you die the Seals are not denied you in spirit. You can receive the Seals now in spirit, in the living flesh, and be free with the Seal because I am who I am.

Try to be Grateful.

Heaven above, Heaven below. For the sake of Love, there we go.

My hope is that Goddess, God, Jesus and the rest will forgive us if we have done a poor job or make a big messianic mess with the disclosure of the Sovereign Seals. If God, Goddess, Jesus and all of the rest are pleased with my work I hope you, the reader, are also pleased with my effort to reveal the Sovereign Seals.

The next books I write will continue along the same vein of Gold, as this book, as we look deeper into our purpose, and our place in the Kingdom of Heaven.

THE END

CPSIA information can be obtained
at www.ICGtesting.com
Printed in the USA
BVHW011724130821
613887BV00007BA/219